To Mead & Alcorn
Tight lines and best regards
Bob Warmy

DON'T BLAME THE FISH

〜〜〜〜〜〜〜〜〜〜〜〜〜〜〜 Winchester Press

DON'T BLAME THE FISH

Bob Warner

Drawings by William B. O'Brian

To Sylvia and Jono,
who head a very long list
of wonderful fishing companions.

"My Life with a Stuffed Sailfish" was previously published
by *Esquire* magazine (June 1939), and "Roughing It"
was previously published by *Rogue* magazine (December 1963).

Library of Congress Catalog Card Number: 73-88871
ISBN: 0-87691-127-0

Book and jacket design by Mary Frances Gazze

Published by Winchester Press
460 Park Avenue, New York 10022

Printed in the United States of America

✍✍✍DON'T
BLAME
THE
FISH

Bob Warner

Drawings by William B. O'Brian

To Sylvia and Jono,
who head a very long list
of wonderful fishing companions.

"My Life with a Stuffed Sailfish" was previously published
by *Esquire* magazine (June 1939), and "Roughing It"
was previously published by *Rogue* magazine (December 1963).

Library of Congress Catalog Card Number: 73-88871
ISBN: 0-87691-127-0

Book and jacket design by Mary Frances Gazze

Published by Winchester Press
460 Park Avenue, New York 10022

Printed in the United States of America

Contents

ᥐᥐᥐ Foreword

On opening day on the Beaverkill forty years ago, my waders leaked, ice formed on the guides of my rod, and suddenly clouds blotted out the sun and it snowed so hard I couldn't see the shore. Trout? Not a suggestion of a trout. So, reluctantly, I quit and went back to the car and there it sat with a flat tire, and, as I shortly learned, an equally flat spare. I had a four-mile hike in that blizzard to the nearest garage.

We who, given the chance, will gladly circumnavigate the globe in hot pursuit of a fish— tarpon, striper, salmon, trout, sailfish, bass, you name it— have all experienced dozens of days as bad or worse, but time blurs the images so they are not the ones we recall. If we did recall them in all their horror we long ago would have given our tackle to our worst enemies and sunk to sailing or playing golf. But we don't. What we re-call, as if it happened almost daily, are those rare occasions in our lives and the lives of others that cannot be appreciated unless you are a fisherman, because no one else would know what you are talking about. These are the occasions that make millionaires out of the brigands who sell us all the rods, reels, flies, and lures we do not really need but buy anyway in the hope that some new gimmick will produce another one of *those days.*

Perhaps the settings in which we function have something to do with all of this. Who would not prefer hiking down a country road in a blizzard to dictating a letter to a salesman about his padded expense account and his incurable habit of making passes at all female prospects under fifty? And thirty feet outside the window is a view of another skyscraper. Yes, the surroundings, the trees, the mountains, the fragrant meadows, the grazing cattle, the dark murmuring water, or the Cape Cod harbor, the roar of pounding surf and the cries of wheeling gulls form the perfect backdrop to man's finest avocation. Forget the old tire or broken toilet seat in the brook, the time you lost your footing and landed head over heels in the ice-cold ocean, or the day you got the hook in your ear; for most of fishing is not like that, most of it is as unspoiled and beautiful as the waters your grandfather fished a hundred years ago. Fishing is the one sport that depends on God's best creative efforts rather than on man's. God's plus a little help from the hatchery.

I caught my first trout sixty-one years ago and my first on a fly two years later, and a year after that landed a striper at Cuttyhunk. In all that time I have failed to fish just one year, 1944, when I was in Southeast Asia, supposedly to make life hard for the Japs. I had brought along my fly rod. What licked me was my full-of-business West-Point-trained commanding officer, who kept insisting that fishing was not why the U. S.

Government had sent me halfway around the world in the midst of a war.

So that gives me sixty years to think about and pick out a limited number of red-letter days to form a fisherman's life, or at least a good part of one. Not an easy task, for looking back almost every day with a rod seems to have had something good about it. Why, even that first day I mentioned. . . . When I finally located a mechanic and a new tire and he finished putting it on, what did he do but dig around in his tool kit and produce a pint of the most magnificent bathtub gin I have ever tasted? (Prohibition! Remember?) That stuff mixed with the murky water of the Beaverkill would have made a professional liquor taster swoon with joy. And to make matters even better it turned out that the mechanic was a fisherman too, so naturally we had to drink the whole bottle.

R. W.

DON'T BLAME THE FISH

ᗦᗦᗦThe Wake

Eb Parsons and I first met Willie Charles at an inn in New
Bedford, Massachusetts, after driving down from Connecticut.
We arrived an hour early for the charter float plane that was
to take us to Wattatuck Island for a few days of striper fishing
with Bill and George Morrison of Hartford, so we repaired to
the inn bar, where we could hear the plane come in, to have a
drink. As we were about to order, a middle-aged guy in fishing
clothes walked in, saw us, also in fishing clothes, and came
over to our table. "You boys aren't headed for Wattatuck by
any chance, are you?"

Eb nodded. "Yuh! Going to meet two chaps camping out
there."

He sat down at our table. "You mean the Morrison brothers? I've never met 'em, but their uncle in New York suggested I join 'em and give 'em some tips on striper fishing. My
name is Willie Charles."

We introduced ourselves and Eb said, "If you can teach George and Bill Morrison anything about striper fishing you must be pretty good. I doubt if there's a fisherman from Boston to Cape May who knows more about striped bass than those boys."

Willie was short, not over five feet six, and his ears stuck out from his crew-cut head like handles on a jug. He must have weighed a hundred and seventy-five pounds and he carried it like a professional hockey player, all muscle.

"Drinks are on me." He called to the bartender, "Three double martinis on the rocks, and make 'em dry."

He glanced at us. "This your first try? Or have you striper-fished before?"

"We've been at it along the New England coast for about fifty years," Eb said.

"Then you know what you're doing. This ought to be a good party. How about a pool, ten dollars each on the biggest fish? Reminds me of a story about New England. Years ago I was fishing Nantucket and I decided to try a new beach. Must have been twenty guys lined up surf casting and not one of 'em had a fish. End of a couple of hours they still didn't have any and I had 'em piled up to my belt, twenty-six if I remember right. You shoulda seen those guys' eyes bug out when I kept takin' 'em every cast.

"So finally I called 'em over and I says, 'Since you fellas don't have any fish I'm going to give each of you one of mine.' That gave me six to take home and that was all I wanted.

"I guess you boys know that to catch stripers you gotta know how to figure your currents and where they lie, and you gotta know how to make long casts. Those guys were okay but they were all about thirty feet short of the fish."

The martinis arrived and Willie took a sip while his eyes

roved over the plump little waitress. "Honey, remind me to give you an extra tip, A for very good martinis, and B because you're a cute little chick."

The waitress giggled and departed.

"Have you ever fished Wattatuck?" Eb asked.

Willie shook his head. "What's Wattatuck mean? Indian word for 'Come on, honey, let's crawl under that bush'?"

I said, "You've got me. But on Wattatuck there isn't a bush high enough for a seagull to crawl under, all sand and grass. Used to be a Coast Guard station there, but a hurricane swept it out to sea."

Willie ordered another round of drinks. When the waitress brought them she leaned way forward over Willie and winked at him. If she had a bra on under her low-necked blouse it wasn't visible, but everything else was. Before she picked up Willie's twenty-dollar bill they had a date for the evening we would return.

When she took off with the money Eb laughed. "If you're that quick with the stripers, heaven help the rest of us."

Willie grinned. "Girls and stripers, my specialties. Work's a bad third."

When we went out to the dock to wait for Bartlett, the pilot who was going to fly us over, we noticed three surf-casting rods among Willie's luggage, and they all looked as if they'd seen plenty of use.

Willie sat up front with Bartlett, because Eb and I had made the flight a dozen times and we wanted him to see the bay and islands en route to Wattatuck. By the time we'd been in the air two minutes Willie was telling the pilot how to fly the plane. Eb and I, and a grim-faced Bartlett, put up with it for about five minutes, then Eb leaned forward and tapped Willie on the shoulder. He said, "Bartlett flew the Hump in

World War II. And he's been a commercial pilot ever since. He can take a plane apart and put it back together with his eyes shut."

We landed in a little bay close to Bill's and George's tents. Willie stuck his head out of the door and yelled, "Hi! Got any fifty-pound stripers, they don't count. Ten-dollar pool starts now." He climbed down onto the float and jumped ashore while we unloaded his and our luggage.

Bartlett, a salty Yankee, said, "If you drown that guy I won't say a thing about bringing him out here."

We arranged for Bartlett to pick us up three days later and watched him shove off, still grumbling about the so-and-sos you occasionally have to carry. We headed up the beach to pitch our tent.

Willie finished erecting his pup tent and straightening out his gear, then said, "Let's give the stripers a chance before lunch. I'll feel better after I nail down that pool. Pretty close to ebb tide."

George said, "Best place to fish now is in a bend a mile and a half up the beach. Won't catch anything in the open ocean off here. Surf is too high."

But Willie was already setting up a rod.

Bill said, "Okay, if he wants exercise. Won't catch a damn thing."

I walked up to the top of the spit and watched Willie, hip deep in the seawater, the surf running right to the tops of his chest waders, sweep his rod back and let go like a tournament caster. I guess I've watched a thousand fishermen surf cast, but the best of the bunch would have been at least twenty-five feet short of Willie. That boy really knew how to handle a rod.

"Soup's on," yelled Eb.

While we were lined up on a driftwood plank in the cook

tent Bill said, "Too bad for that guy to miss a hot lunch. I've fished here about forty times and I've never taken a striper or a blue off that beach."

"Kind of a queer duck," said George. "Wonder where Uncle Harry ever ran into him?"

Fifteen minutes later while we were drinking coffee Willie called outside the tent, "Any food left?"

"Sure! Come and get it. How'd you make out?"

"Okay! Got one fair one." He came into the cook tent and sat down. "Don't have a drink, do you? Forgot to bring mine. Boy, I'm parched."

I fished out a bottle of Scotch and Eb went outside to see what he'd gotten. A second later he called, "Hey, you guys, come out here and bring the scale."

The striper weighed thirty-eight pounds, a one-in-a-hundred fish for Wattatuck.

"Call that big?" said Willie. "Fifty pounds up is what I'm after. Reminds me of the time I shared a tent with a guy's wife on Martha's Vineyard. The guy was so grateful to me for showing him how to catch stripers he said he wanted to do something for me, and the only thing he could think of was to give me his beautiful wife for the night. He went off and slept under a tree. In the morning she crawled out of bed and said, "Phew! I'm not going to be able to walk straight for two days. If you're as good with the stripers as you are in the sack you're the world's best fisherman."

At this point I was beginning to thank heaven the trip was only going to last three days.

Later in the afternoon we all fished the westward side of the island. The stripers were either elsewhere or around and not cooperating. Then, finally, at four o'clock I hooked a nice one, fly casting, of around twenty pounds. Next thing I knew Willie had waded out and was right beside me, shouting instructions at the top of his lungs.

"Hold your rod up!" My rod tip was up, but he grabbed it and forced it back almost to the breaking point. "Put your drag on! Don't let your fish run that way! Goddammit, put the drag on! You're going to lose that fish! Here, give me your rod!" And he tried to yank it out of my hands. Happily I was bigger than Willie, so in spite of a partially crippled shoulder and a bum arm I hung on.

"Christ's sake, that's no way to fish. How many times do I have to tell you to put that drag on?"

The reel was a salmon reel and the drag was on, full. I told him this, but he shouted, "Don't tell me about reels," then leaned in front of me and threw the drag off. The fish yanked off about twenty feet of line, backlashed the line, and broke the leader.

"Thanks!" I said. "I don't know what I would have done without you."

"Goddammit, if you'da let me take your rod . . . All I can say is it's a good thing I came along."

I glanced down. The gaff that Willie wore in his belt had cut a gash ten inches long in my waders, too long to repair on Wattatuck. My bad arm and shoulder ached from the struggle to hang onto my rod. I staggered ashore with my water-filled boot, leaned my rod against a rock to keep sand out of the reel, the tip in the beach grass, and sat down to have a smoke.

Willie followed me up the shore. "Got another cigarette?" he asked. As he reached me he stepped on my $250 Orvis salmon rod and broke the butt joint in two. He looked at it. "Guess it's cracked a little. Too bad. You can splice it. But that fly rod's no good for stripers anyway. Much too light. Here, give me a cigarette."

And that and three stripers that Bill caught were the only ones hooked that afternoon.

After supper and a lot more tales of Willie always landing next to the biggest fish in the world wherever he was and whatever he was fishing for, the wind changed and came straight out of the north. George finally managed to get a word in. "Tide will turn in thirty minutes, just before dark. With this wind there's just one place to fish, Virgins' Point. There's a narrow shelf and a steep drop-off, and the tide rips through there a mile a minute, so don't wade more than knee deep. Anyone steps off the edge of that shelf the chances of getting him out alive are pretty close to zero."

Willie helped himself to a drink of our whiskey and said, "Don't worry. This old man knows how to take care of himself. Tide rips don't mean a thing to me— I seen too many of 'em."

George looked at him. "Suit yourself. I just didn't want Uncle Harry to think we drowned you."

"That reminds me of a story about a beautiful redhead." There was a low groan but Willie didn't hear it.

Eb had loaned me another rod and I was going to fish without waders, and in a very sour temper.

By the time we reached Virgins' Point it was dark and we fished by moonlight. The tide rip was boiling and made a deep, Niagara-like roar. But we all started getting stripers and blues on almost every cast. If it hadn't been for Willie's running comments it would have been perfect.

Then it happened. But not the way you think.

Willie was wading almost up to his belt, much too far out for safety. "Look out, Willie," Eb shouted. "Back up. You're much too close to the edge. That drops off into seven or eight feet of water."

"Quiet," said Willie. "Don't tell me how to wade."

Just then Willie hooked a huge striper. It surfaced in the moonlight and we all saw it. It was the best one any of us had tied into, and of course Willie was yelling how this would put us all to shame when suddenly his line started going out as though he'd harpooned a whale. We all stopped fishing to watch. Bill said, "Hard to believe, but I think something has taken that striper."

Willie shouted above the roar of the surf. "Guess you're about to see another world's record. Fishing experts, shove over and watch Willie Charles perform."

Then even Willie, realizing that he had nothing average on his line, shut up. He was fishing with a big two-handed salt-water casting rod, and the line went off the reel so fast he could hardly hold the rod, which was now pointing in a straight line between him and the fish.

The fish turned and rolled, and in the moonlight we saw its dorsal fin and long back. I swear, and the others agree, that the damned fish must have been at least thirty feet long. What in God's name was it, a killer whale off course, or a great white shark even farther from home? The fish finished its roll and idled slowly shoreward, combatting the fierce tide rip racing by the point. Still in deep water, it raised its huge head and spat out Willie's very large striper the way a pike would spit out a small artificial frog, then turned slowly to swim out to sea. As it swung, still fighting the tide, its tail struck Willie and knocked him off the shelf into deep water and that wildly churning rip. The fish came around in a tight circle, saw Willie struggling, and opened its huge jaws. I've never seen bait taken head first in a nicer fashion. Willie disappeared. But, big as the fish was, it couldn't get him down in a single swallow. Once again it raised its head above the water and we

could see Willie's wader-clad feet sticking out of each side of its cavernous mouth. Then it dove and took off for deep water.

"My God!" Eb gasped. "I can't believe it."

George said, "Come on, we gotta get the Coast Guard."

"How you going to get 'em?" Bill asked. "No house, no boat, no phone on this island. What are we going to do, swim five miles to Chappaquiddick?"

"My God!" George murmured.

Suddenly it came home to all of us. We stood there in the yellow light of the moon, gazing in stunned silence at the water where Willie had disappeared. We all tried to think of something— anything— to do.

"It's awful quiet around here— too quiet," Bill said. "We have to do something."

"I suggest we go back to camp and have a wake," George said. "Seems to me that's the least we can do. It's a good thing you guys, Bill and I each packed whiskey for the whole crowd. It's likely to be kind of a long wake. No sense in hanging around here."

We strung our stripers and blues, put them over our shoulders, and, single-file behind Eb's flashlight, trooped in silence the mile back to camp. There we lit the kerosene lamp, and got ice out of the fish box, and each of us poured a glass full of straight whiskey.

Sitting on the heavy plank in the cook tent, we drank in silence. The roar of the surf seemed deafening.

Finally Bill said, "Okay! Any of you guys ever had any experience running a wake?"

No one had.

Bill said, "Least we can do is think of something nice to say about the guy. Bob, say something."

I thought hard. Then, "Sure hope that fish doesn't have

trouble digesting his waders. Eight pounds of rubber is quite a lot for the alimentary canal. It would be a pity if the fish got sick."

"Boy, I'd sure like to catch a fish that size," volunteered Eb. "Trouble is our bait's gone. We should have had a hook fastened to him."

We all poured another drink. Bill said, "You guys aren't trying. There must have been something nice about that bastard. After all, he's dead."

"I just had a horrible thought," George said. "Remember the way that fish spit out the striper? What if he spits Willie out the same way and he makes it back to shore?"

It was a chilling thought. We all refilled our glasses. "In that tide rip?" Eb said. "Not a chance." We felt better. Everyone took a long drink.

"Come on, you guys, this is a hell of a wake," Bill said. "After all, the guy was human."

I refilled my glass for the fourth time. I said, "Why don't we take a vote?"

The vote was three to one that Willie wasn't. "Guess I'd like to change my vote," Bill said. "Seems to me we ought to make it unanimous."

Three days later Bartlett came back and found us still stretched out on the beach, trying to recover from the last bottle.

"You guys all in the booze?" Bartlett asked.

"We been waking. I mean holding a wake. Everything is very sad," said George.

"Where's the other guy, the one who was teaching me how to fly?" asked Bartlett.

"Fish got him," Bill said.

Bartlett roared with laughter. "I don't blame the fish. But

seriously, who do you think is ever going to believe that? Take that story into court and they'll hang the four of you."

So we changed it. When the Coast Guard and the cops arrived we told how we had warned Willie about the deep water at the edge of the shelf but he'd paid no attention and had been swept away in the tide rip. For two weeks the Coast Guard had a sizable fleet of boats searching for the remains, but they never found a thing. Not even a wader shoe.

~~~One of Concord's Famous

Concord, Massachusetts, is famous for several things: the battle by the rude bridge that arched the flood, the Concord grape, Ralph Waldo Emerson, Henry David Thoreau, Louisa May Alcott, and me.

I was nine years old and my father had taken me fishing in a Model T Ford driven by his tough Swedish chauffeur, Jonas, a man who had always had my number. Father told Jonas to stop the car a few rods before a bridge that spanned the upper end of a large pool.

Father said, "Now you stand right here, Robert, and watch me and I'll show you how to fish this pool." (I later taught my sons in the same fashion.) He approached the pool through the long grass, crouched over so as not to put his shadow on it, and knelt down on the bank and worked every square foot of it until he was convinced there wasn't a fish in it. Then he crawled back and said, "Now that is the way I want you to do it. You fish here and I'll work downstream." And he departed hopefully for more productive water.

Jonas hauled a wad of chewing tobacco out of his pocket, bit off about a quarter of a pound, and marched out onto the bridge, sending his shadow the pool's full length.

"You heard what Father said," said I in my most threatening manner.

"Huh!" he snorted, after looking downstream to make sure Father was out of earshot. He fired about half a cuspidor full of tobacco juice in a long arc to the pool's center, where it landed as delicately as a falling meteor.

"I'm going to tell," I said as I joined him.

"Huh!" he announced again. "You mean about you putting a snake in the cook's bed, or your fight with the McGuire kid yesterday?"

As I said, he had my number.

I stripped off my heavy untapered line, made a few casts I hoped could be described as false casts, then let go. The curled line landed in the water with a loud plop and the large wet fly, attached to the heaviest gut my father owned, sank down out of sight, right to the bottom of the pool. I retrieved slowly, not paying much attention to my fishing, my mind preoccupied with the problem of how to get Jonas sacked. Suddenly I was aware that something was at the other end of my line. I let him have it with a strike that was just about right for nine hundred pounds of black marlin.

"You got one," Jonas shouted. "Give me your rod, I'll help you."

"You go to hell," I shouted back in the cultivated vocabulary of a properly raised young Bostonian.

I ran off the bridge and down the bank to be closer to whatever it was that had taken my fly. The fish shot down the pool so fast that it backlashed my reel and almost yanked the rod out of my hands. There was just one thing to do, and I did it. I put the rod over my shoulder and marched up the bank. Jonas grabbed the line and helped pull. No trout was ever better hooked. This one left the stream and flapped its way two yards from the water's edge. Jonas and I both made dives to grab it before it could flop back into the stream. I got there first. A trout— an enormous brook trout.

I heard my father shout from the other side of the bridge. "What's happened? Has Robert fallen in? Jonas, where are you?"

I glanced up at Jonas. His face was the color of wet ashes and tears streamed from his eyes. He mumbled a word that even in these days of enlightened censorship had best not be repeated, then added, "I swallowed my chew." After which he and his breakfast parted company. Father had to drive the Ford home because Jonas was too sick to hold the wheel. He sat there by himself on the back seat, groaning and upchucking over the side, maintaining me in a state of absolute bliss.

The trout weighed four and three-quarters pounds, at least twice as big as any of the oldest residents had ever heard of being taken from a Concord brook. Now most of its dorsal fin has departed and much of the paint has chipped off its lower jaw, but it still hangs on the wall above my desk to remind me that I am one of Concord's greats.

ᔇᔇᔇFlies
and Hooks Astray

The first time I heard a story about someone getting a fly in his eyelid I thought it was pretty funny. The second time there was nothing funny about it.

The late Sam Anderson, an Assistant Secretary of Commerce, told me of accident one. He was salmon fishing with a friend in Ireland. A high wind was blowing and casting was very difficult; lines and flies whipped every which way. They stuck at it for hours, or until Sam's companion sank a fly well over the barb in his eyelid.

Sam cut the leader, helped the fisherman into the car and raced to the small village nearby in search of a doctor. The fisherman was bleeding badly and in extreme pain. Sam said nothing but he was afraid the eye was a goner.

After lengthy conversations with a number of Irishmen, who are always glad for a chance to talk to pass the time of day, a pair of men, very sober in spite of a generous amount of whiskey before lunch, located the only doctor's office in the area. An elderly white-haired lady in a nurse's uniform opened the door.

"We need to see the doctor immediately. This is an emergency," Sam said.

"Himself is not here. He's out deliverin' another sucklin'—what Ireland needs the least."

"Can we get him on the phone?"

"No, and you can't. For sure and how would I know whose brat he's bringin'? This may not be much of a town but there's nothin' special about the young potwallopers havin' brats in it. They're up to it all o' the while, and many o' them not six months from the altar. If I was his Holiness I'd refuse to christen the lot o' them. The doctor will be back anon unless the hussy called him afore her time. Here, come in under the light. I'm a nurse, mayhap I can help ye.

"Sit here," she said. "I'll be for adjustin' the light." She leaned over Sam's friend and said, "Hmm!" Then she went to the medicine closet and fetched a magnifying glass. She studied the situation a long while, then sniffed in disdain. "For sure and that's a Green Highlander. A fly o' some value perhaps in Scotland, where the salmon are all the size o' the smelt and scrawny, and where the Scotch know not the first thing about fishin', among a great many other things they know nothin' of, but a fly o' no value here where the fish like the fishermen are o' fine intelligence and come sturdy and big. If I was doin' it I'd be for tryin' a Mar Lodge or a Jock Scott."

Sam's temptation to strangle her was interrupted by the doctor's arrival. "Damn girl had twins," he grumbled, coming

$\mathcal{R}\mathcal{R}\mathcal{R}$ Flies and Hooks Astray

around a corner. "And I strongly suspect neither one will be resemblin' the husband. Ah! And what have we here?"

In a matter of seconds he had the hook out. "No damage done," he said, "but to guard against infection I'll put a bandage on. And I suggest you now stop fishin' in this gale and take to the whiskey bottle until the morrow. Good Irish whiskey never hurt any man, so long as he stopped for the day at the end o' the first bottle, which few o' them do unless their money's run out."

The second occasion took place on Vermont's Batten Kill. My wife, Sylvia, and Jono, my oldest boy, then a freshman at Yale, had heard me talk so much about this beloved river that they had persuaded me to take them there for a weekend. The river was very high, and most of it much too deep for Sylvia to wade. So I suggested she put on a dry fly and fish up from the bridge toward Manchester Center, where the water would be hip-deep with a firm gravel bottom and an almost treeless meadow on one side that would make casting easy. I told her to tie on a Hendrickson on a #16 hook. Then Jono and I walked a mile downstream into the woods where the deeper pools lay.

Two hours later, when we returned, Sylvia was standing on the bridge, the #16 Hendrickson hook sunk over the barb in her eyelid.

"My God! Come on, let's find a doctor. Maybe I ought to take you to Bennington to the hospital," I said.

"Don't be crazy," responded Sylvia. "I've already located a doctor, Campbell in Manchester Center. He sounds nice and Vermonty, like Calvin Coolidge. I walked up to the drug store and telephoned. The druggist recommended him."

"Why didn't you take the car and go to him?" Jono asked.

"Because your dad had the keys in his pocket. I thought of

taking a taxi, but then I was afraid that you two would come back and find me missing and all sorts of wild ideas would go galloping through your dad's skull."

"This is awful," I said. "Let's get out of here. Quick."

Sylvia looked at Jono. "See what I mean?"

Dr. Campbell glanced at the fly and like all doctors everywhere said, "Hmm!" Then he said, "Got a pair of cuttin' pliers in your tackle kit? I'm goin' to bring the barb up through and cut the end of the hook off."

Of course I didn't have them. At least not then. Needless to say, since then . . . "Does it hurt much, dear?" I asked.

Sylvia shook her head. "Not much, though I don't think I'd care to wear it permanently. At least it's giving me a fish's view of things."

The doctor disappeared and returned with a vicious-looking piece of slaughterhouse equipment, long heavy handles and knifelike blades that could have cut an oak in two. He held them close to Sylvia's eye. She shrank back.

I said, "Jumping H. Jesus!" and cleared the floor by two feet.

Jono, a quiet scholarly kid, said in a whisper, "Dad, I think you were right about the Bennington Hospital. How far is it?"

Sylvia glanced at the portable guillotine and said, "Goodbye everybody. Up until now it was fun."

Dr. Campbell looked at the Hendrickson nestled in Sylvia's eye, then at his dainty optical equipment. "Reckon these are a little large," he said— Vermont's record understatement for that year. "These are for dehornin' cattle; I figured they might cut that hook, bein' we got no pliers. Since it's Sunday all the garages are closed." He looked at me. "You know the Orvis tackle people?"

"Most of them," I answered. "I used to live in Manchester."

"Go see if you can find one at home to open the shop. I'll try the jeweler. He lives over his store. If you can't get into Orvis and the jeweler's not there, I'll throw a rock through the front window and get in that way." He looked at me, hard. "You willin' to pay for a new plate-glass window? Could cost you a pack 'o money."

"Don't worry," I said. "Bust it."

Jono stayed with Sylvia while the doctor and I raced off in opposite directions. But I could rouse none of the Orvis Company. Finally I had to give up and drove back to the doctor's. He entered his driveway about two seconds later. "No problem," he shouted. "Jeweler was home."

"Thank heaven!" I said. "Doctor, tell me, is this serious?"

"Serious! Hell no. Shoulda seen the one I got last week. Hook about ten times the size of that little thing she was usin'. Had seven angleworms attached to it. Like tryin' to get a hook out of a dish of spaghetti."

A half-hour later we were all fishing again.

⚘⚘⚘The Honeymoon

Back in 1955, George Poindexter was twenty-four and Mabel
Butterly twenty-one. 1955! Those were the days when kids
who developed an interest in each other didn't pop into bed
after the second kiss but waited until the bride went through
the pageantry of marching down the aisle on her old man's
arm (cost: fifty bucks a step for him by the time he cleaned up
the bills), preceded by the ushers laying down a thick haze of
Scotch mist. In those days things were done correctly. And it
wasn't because kids weren't just as eager to get between the
sheets as today's young. They were. But that, of course, was
before the pill, when it was comparatively easy for parents to
scare a daughter out of a year's growth by warning her of what
would happen if she clambered under a bush before saying
"I do."

Mabel and George were both working in Washington,

D. C., she as a secretary for a government agency that dealt in internal, external, vertical, and horizontal confusion called the C. I. A., where she typed up papers labeled HUSH, CONFIDENTIAL, EYES ALONE, TOP SECRET— mostly stuff that had appeared in the New York *Times* three days earlier. George labored for the Department of Commerce trying to find something to do that would keep him from dropping dead of boredom. He had been there ever since graduating from college three years earlier and making the mistake of listening to a Commerce Department recruiting officer, who made a clerk's job in that institution sound like the adventures of Marco Polo. He had a foot-long title, but to date no one had invented a job to go with it. His problem was not the department's fault; they had suddenly been faced with the necessity, at the end of their fiscal year, of putting three hundred and eighty-seven people they didn't need on their payroll, or being faced with a large surplus and the odious task of admitting to Congress that they were getting umpteen million dollars of the taxpayers' dough they didn't know how to spend.

So George shot flies with rolled-up bits of paper and a rubber band and spent a great deal of time doing research in the department's aquarium, where he gave particular attention to the trout and bass and to dreaming of a river where he could catch some like them. Some people are born with silver spoons in their mouths, but not George. He had entered the world with his tiny jaws clamped on a bass plug.

For three months George and Mabel spent five days a week in their offices and every evening from eight to eleven necking on various side streets in George's car. Saturdays and Sundays they took picnic lunches and went into the country to neck, except during the trout season when George explained that he had to go to New York to see a sick aunt. He did not have the courage right at that time to tell Mabel that while he loved to neck he also liked to fish. While George had never set any academic records on fire he was still smart enough to know that Mabel's reply would be a pouting, "You mean you'd rather catch a slimy old fish than kiss me?"

Finally, one evening, George asked, "Will you marry me?" and she stopped chewing his ear long enough to reply, "Yes, darling, of course."

George, who had started fishing at the age of four, suggested that it might be fun to go to northern Ontario and camp out, and perhaps wet a line or two on their honeymoon.

"No," Mabel said. "I want to go to Nag's Head in North Carolina and see the dune where the Wright brothers took off." She glanced hastily out of the car window to make sure no one was listening, because she had a strong suspicion that the Wright brothers' flight was still classified information. "And besides, I want my first tumble in the hay on an innerspring mattress, not with a lot of wolves and polar bears trying to pull the tent down."

George finally agreed. After all, they would use only half their vacation time on their honeymoon. And in September, when the big Canadian brookies were starting their spawning runs . . .

Then came the wedding, and they drove down to the night boat for Norfolk. Happily they made the boat with time to spare, because when they got there they discovered their tickets were back in George's apartment in another suit. They made the boat a second time with roughly thirty seconds to get their car on board.

At last they closed the door of the honeymoon suite and he took her in his arms, one eye gazing lustfully over her head at that beautiful double bed. He started unbuttoning her blouse.

There was a loud hissing sound, followed by a louder bang as a piece of pipe hit the wall, and suddenly they were in a cloud of steam. It was burning hot, so thick they couldn't see each other, and their brand-new going-away clothes were as wet as if they had started married life in a shower. They groped their way to the door and unlocked it. As they swung it open the cloud of steam followed them into the corridor.

After a frantic search George located the third mate, who said he would look into it as soon as the boat was out in the current. "Must have something to do with a steam pipe," he added brightly, and now please let him tend this ship.

So they let him tend the ship, if looking over the railing at two mating sea gulls could be called tending it, until it was in the middle of the Potomac going full speed downstream.

"Now about that busted pipe?" Mabel asked.

"Ah, yes, the pipe," he answered. "I'll have a look at it." He rolled on ahead of them in his practiced seadog gate. This was his second overnight cruise since completing his correspondence course on how to become a ship's officer. Already he was twice as salty as Joseph Conrad.

He stuck his head in the door and pulled it out. "Lot of steam in there."

The upshot was, of course, that the guy who knew how to fix steam pipes was on shore— whether on leave or just because he was smart George and Mabel never learned.

The correspondence-school mate did what he admitted was "kind o' a patch-up job," with some old rags and a ball of string. At least the steam no longer whistled as it left the pipe, but the cabin was still wet enough to have drowned a duck and a foghorn would have been needed for anyone to find the bathroom.

All other rooms were taken, so George and Mabel spent the

night in the lounge. "Oh dear!" she wailed. "Our bags! We ought to get them out of there."

The bags were so full of water that George had to haul them out one at a time. Everything was drenched. He sighed. "If only we had gills we could set up housekeeping in a pond."

"You and your idea of what's funny," she said and burst into tears.

So they sat in the lounge all night and necked, when Mabel wasn't sobbing over her ruined trousseau. The next morning, looking like a couple of stowaways who had had to swim ashore, they splashed down the gangplank and drove to Nag's Head.

"First, let's find a dry cleaner and a laundry," Mabel said.

"Mmm!" George answered, paying no attention. He had just spotted two men with long surf-casting rods over their shoulders. "What do you suppose they fish for here?" he asked.

She sniffled. "My silk things are absolutely ruined. We'll have to sue the steamship company. What did you say?"

"I said, what kind of fish do you suppose they catch here?"

"Something called a striped bass. It was in the folder the inn sent. I forgot to tell you. Ohhh! My clothes . . ." She was off again.

Then came one of those rare wonderful breaks that make life worth the fuss. They located a dry-cleaning and laundry establishment offering twenty-four-hour service, and right next door was a tackle store.

George carried the bags into the first shop and said to Mabel, "Please have everything I own dry-cleaned and laundered except my razor. You'll find me next door."

"Where are you going?" she asked.

"I'm looking for the men's room," he answered and was off.

A half-hour later when she joined him he was richer by a

hundred-and-twenty-six-dollar surf-casting outfit, including a pile of hardware claimed to be irresistible to stripers. "Now what you do," the clerk told him, "is to cast beyond the breakers. Stripers aren't running right now, but you can always pick up the odd one. Too bad you weren't here last week."

But at least he was going to fish. He had never caught a striper. He trembled with anticipation. And here they occasionally got them up to fifty pounds. . . . This honeymoon was turning out okay after all, in spite of their soggy clothes.

"Come on," Mabel said. "I want a swim. Not that I've been doing much else since we got on that damned boat."

At the inn Mabel wrung out her bathing suit and donned it in the bathroom (after all, it wasn't time for him to look yet— first he had to get his mind off that rod and all that junk). No bikini; she had brought along a full suit. When George got his first glimpse she wanted him to have the works— no installment-plan stuff. She picked up a book with the pages all stuck together and a large inn towel. George packed up his tackle and they headed for the beach.

"Why don't you put on your bathing suit?" she asked.

"I won't need it. I'm going to cast from the shore."

On the beach George looked out at the breakers. There were rows and rows of breakers. He tied on a heavy plug and let go. Not far enough. He could barely get beyond the first five rows of white water. Ah well, his new sport jacket and slacks were wet anyway. He stepped into the water, turning to glance at his bride, expecting a howl of protest. But she was out flat on the sand, reading away in the broiling sun.

He cast again. Still was short. What the hell! He waded in, knee deep.

Mabel looked up and down the beach. Not a soul in sight. They had it all to themselves. She sat up and peeled off her

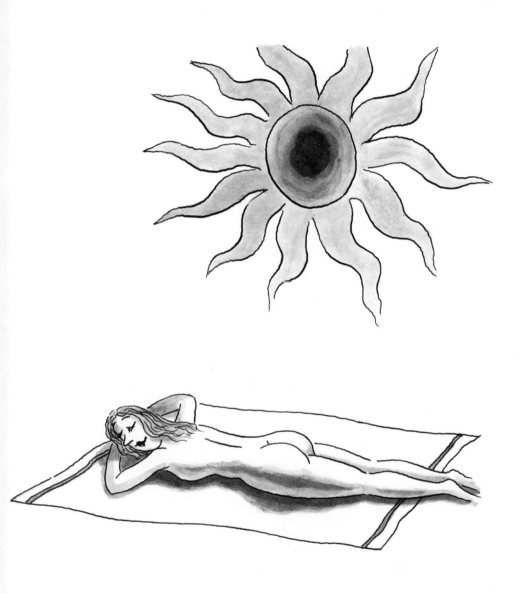

bathing suit. While she wasn't opposed to a uniform tanning job, this was not the reason for the strip. Mabel felt that the time was *now* to stir her husband's blood and get his mind off fish. And as long as no one was around there really wasn't anything wrong with this towel. She'd bet lots of girls had been had in worse places. She tried a couple of seductive wiggles to bring her quarry in.

It got her nowhere. George had his mind on other things— how to get beyond that outer breaker where presumably the stripers lay. This was quite an undertaking, because the breakers seemed to stretch about halfway to Spain.

The first time Mabel realized she wasn't making any headway was when she looked around and couldn't find George. Then she saw him, just as a wave rolled over his head and took off his hat. He still was twenty feet short of that last breaker.

Finally Mabel threw in the sponge and put her suit on. Minutes later George waded ashore. "My God!" he said to her. "You look like a broiled lobster. Thank goodness that suit covers most of you."

She began to cry. "I just put it back on. I'm hot all over. And you never looked at me once. You're a brute. I wish I hadn't married you."

As they rounded a curve in the beach they came on five fishermen after stripers. Two were sitting on wooden boxes, the others were standing— all comfortable, dry, and on shore. They were all casting, just beyond the first breaker about twenty feet out. And two of them had fish.

An hour later the inn located a doctor. After looking Mabel over he gave George a large jar of sulphurous yellow salve that stained everything, and said, "Keep her covered with this, and put it on gently. Why you city folks never learn is beyond me. She's got a first-class burn, and it's going to be a lot worse before it's better. I suggest you give up skin diving, or whatever you've been doing in your slacks and sport jacket, and stay right here with her. Get the inn to fill this prescription. It's codeine for the pain. And put an ice bag on her head; she's going to run a temperature. I'll be back this evening."

When George touched her, no matter how gently, she moaned with pain. At the end of the second day she began to peel and the pain was worse.

At the end of a week they went home. Mabel was well padded with yellow grease and cheesecloth and looked about as sexy as something out of an Egyptian tomb. Their honeymoon was over and she could boast, as few ladies can, that she wound it up still a virgin. And so did George, at least so far as striped bass were concerned. But he and Mabel somewhere along the line got to doing better— at last count they had three kids. And Mabel learned how to fish. And now she's a complete addict. Their first child, a boy, is named Salmo Salar Poindexter; the second, a girl, Parmachene Belle; and the last, another boy, Mabel named after a return trip to Nag's Head where she landed a forty-six-pound striper, her first. That night to celebrate she and George drank champagne and manufactured little Roccus Saxatilis in the same bed where she had spent her honeymoon. They chose the Latin name because George insisted that Striped Bass Poindexter sounded a little thick.

ᔰᔰ My Life
with a Stuffed Sailfish

If Andrew Jackson hadn't waded in and attached Florida to
the Union there would now be an awful depression in the
warehouse industry. To the man who introduced hobnails and
cigar butts to the White House floors, the storage business
owes a debt it will never pay. Warehouses put up a wide vari-
ety of stuff: baby carriages, bureaus from the room of the van-
ished maid, photoengravings, moth-eaten deer heads, and so
on. These articles, which come from all over the United
States, are good but transient— in other words, no staying
power. Baby carriages are hauled out and employed for more
babies, the bureaus go up to Yale, photoengravings are given
to a nice old aunt in St. Louis who has never learned how to

say no, and deer heads wind up in barber shops with sad expressions in their glass eyes and hats on their antlers. Dependable is what these things are not; they're like railroad securities, they come and go and eventually— like a bat out of hell— they're gone forever. So if you are a banker preparing to make a loan on one of these gaunt edifices, there is only one way to be absolutely safe: go through it and count the stuffed sailfish. When one of these Palm Beach to Miami creatures passes into storage he's there for good— as much a part of the place as the dust on the basement floor.

The day George got back from Florida and came piling into my office rubbing his hands together and saying "Ahh!" I prepared to explain this to him, because I saw right away what had happened. They are always like that at first— as though they've just swallowed the canary, or been asked to serve in the cabinet.

I said, "George, did you content yourself with having the damned thing photographed?"

He sat on the corner of my desk and took a deep breath. "Listen, Bob, wait till I tell you—"

"Don't," I said. "I already know. You caught a sailfish and are going to have it stuffed."

He said, "Gosh! How'd you hear about it? Of course, the papers. Know what I'm going to do? I'm going to give it to Edith for Christmas. Boy, won't she be surprised! She doesn't even know it's being mounted."

I nodded. "She'll be surprised all right. That's one thing you can count on. If you live from now until the sun turns into an ice cube you'll never forget the look that's going to spread itself over Edith's face when you inform her that instead of getting that winter coat she's after she's to be presented with a

stuffed fish. Even now when I remember breaking the news to Sylvia it makes me feel as though I had just fallen out the window."

"Oh!" he said, in a very dejected manner. "So you caught one too? I suppose yours was a small one."

I sighed. "If only it had been. Believe me, when you have a thing like that pursuing you through life every inch is something to remember. Unfortunately mine is seven feet ten. As far as I can find out they're all seven feet ten except when caught by Lee Wulff and Joe Brooks. It must be the stock size."

"Know how many times mine jumped?" he inquired.

I said, "It's not important— at least not as long as it didn't have the decency to jump off the hook and stay where it belonged."

George said, "You should have seen the last run he made. I had him right alongside—"

"I know," I interrupted, "when he took one look at you and the boat and turned around and hauled out a quarter of a mile of line. They always do it; it's in their contract."

"Captain said he'd never seen anything like it in all the years he's been going out. Said when it swung around and started out to sea that way he'd have given fifty-to-one odds against my catching it."

I groaned. "Those were my captain's exact words. And after that, when they have you thinking that what you really ought to do is go on a lecture tour and write books about yourself, they rush you in and introduce you to the taxidermist, who tells you your fish is one of the finest specimens he's ever seen and would you mind letting him have it for the Museum of Natural History. At that instant it comes over you that the one thing you can't do is part with this acquisition, so you sign up for a Grade A mounting job. And then get your fish hung up and have a lot of pictures taken at ten dollars per while they go home and divide up the spoils. George, for goodness sake wire that guy you're about to file a petition for bankruptcy and ask him if he'll settle for fifty bucks and keep the fish."

"Look," said George, handing me a photograph of himself and catch. "What do you think of it? Pretty good, don't you agree?"

"Magnificent," I said. "Now then, the thing to do is to have it made into a Christmas card and send it to everyone you know, and stop there. It's enough. If you don't believe it ask my wife, or your wife, or ask the man who owns one."

He put his hands behind his back and gazed up at the ceiling. "I suppose the best place for it will be on the north wall."

"You mean," I inquired, "the one where the portrait of old General What's-his-name, Edith's grandfather, now hangs? I suppose she'll be pretty happy when you tell her that picture has to go in the closet."

George said, "It is kind of a problem. If the picture weren't so darned big we might put it in the bedroom."

"Why don't you cut it in half?" I suggested. "You could throw the legs away and just keep the top part. Or better still, you might slide the whole thing under the bed. Then when Edith wanted to show it to someone she could get down on her hands and knees and use a flashlight."

George said, "By the way, Bob, do these taxidermist guys demand the whole two hundred and fifty bucks on delivery?"

I shook my head. "No indeed, they're very obliging. I took six months with mine. Matter of fact, it's a good idea to pay for 'em catch as catch can— kind of gets you warmed up to your life's work."

"What do you mean, 'life's work'?" he asked.

"You surely didn't think the stuffing bill was the end of it? That's just an introduction to the business. There's the express charge— twenty-five dollars. Then you discover the plaster isn't strong enough to hold your glass-eyed friend, so you have to have a carpenter come in and do all kinds of stuff to the wall. He charges you fifty dollars, and when you move he comes back and charges you forty more to make the place the way it used to be. On top of that he gets thirty-five dollars for building a crate so you can move your piscatorial pal and have him arrive in one piece."

George said, "I wish Edith hadn't put those chartreuse curtains in the living room. Chartreuse and blue . . . Hmm! Perhaps it'll work, though."

"And there's your Louis XIV furniture," I added. "Nothing like a stuffed sailfish to set off brocade and gilt."

"Oh, by the way, Bob, there's another thing I wanted to ask you. How much ceiling height do you need? Our living room's only ten feet."

"That's plenty," I assured him. "That should put his tail about one inch above the sofa. And if it's not enough you can bore a hole in the ceiling and have him sheathe his sword. We only had nine feet in our first apartment."

"How'd you work it?" he asked.

"Easy. We kept the fish in a vacant apartment. Only cost us eight dollars a month."

George laughed. "Just wait till Charlie Wade sees it. Boy, oh boy! Him and his five-pound brown trout." He reached out and retrieved the photograph of himself and fish and gazed at it as if he and the fish were planning to be married on the first of the month. Then he climbed off the desk. "So long," he said. "I suppose I'd better go do some work."

"Nice to have seen you, George. And listen, old man, I

really am sorry. By the way, better let me give you the name of that warehouse; they'll board your fish for a dollar a month less than anyone else in the city. They've had mine for nine years."

"Did you know they have to paint them entirely by hand?" he asked. "The minute they die they start losing their color."

I said, "Yes, I know." A couple of minutes later I glanced up and saw him in the outer office. He was showing his photograph to the girl at the information desk.

♪♪♪Assinica Trout

About a dozen years ago Jono finished his first three years at M. I. T., working on his doctorate in biophysics. He had completed his classes and research and for the past year had been involved with his thesis. There is an unwritten gentleman's agreement that when you start on a project of this kind you must publish the subject of your thesis and research problem so that two scientists will not duplicate each other's efforts. Jono had done so and had spent a year of very hard work when another scientist announced that he had achieved the goal Jono had been aiming for. The other man had neglected to let the world of science know what he was doing. That meant that Jono had to develop a new project and start all over again.

When I met him that summer at Chibougamau, a hundred and fifty miles north of Quebec's Lake St. John, he was under-

standably low in spirits, and seemed very tired and lacked his normal enthusiasm for trout fishing.

It is a short flight, only sixty miles, from Cache Lake, the bush airline base at Chibougamau, to Lake Assinica and the Broadback River. But it took us three days of his five-day holiday to make it because of a heavy fog. Three days of sitting around a French Canadian bush airline office is well on the short side of paradise, even if you are not depressed to start with. The reading material was all in French and consisted of old copies of aviation magazines and about fifty back issues of the French equivalent of our *Police Gazette.* By the end of the first day we both had had enough of flying machines and undraped females to last us the rest of our days.

Finally, at five-thirty on the afternoon of our third day, the fog lifted enough for us to take off. We arrived at the Lake Assinica camp just in time for dinner. When we walked into the dining room Ron Thierry, the camp owner, whom I have known for years, announced to the gathered fishermen, "This is Bob Warner and his son, Jono. They are two of the best fly fishermen in America. Now you guys are going to see some trout."

This over-large statement made me realize that Ron was trying to lift the drooping spirits of a lot of fishermen who obviously had been catching nothing. It did not sound very good.

The next morning we crossed the short stretch of water between the island where the camp stood to the start of the Broadback. The Indian guide beached the canoe, and we fished the wide river from the boulder-lined shores.

By the time we quit for lunch we had not even seen a trout. We had tried at least twenty-five streamer and marabou patterns. Back on the river, Jono said, "Dad, if they would take these big flies they would also take the hardware most of these guys are using. And they aren't catching anything either. Don't you have some small wet flies? Or better, nymphs?"

I shook my head. Then I remembered that by mistake I had included a box of English trout flies, patterns I had never seen before. They had been sent to me earlier that summer by Thomas Hardy & Sons as a gift because a clerk had made an error in a shipment I had ordered.

The fly Jono selected had a mottled gray-and-black wing, a dark-gray woolly body, and gray hackles. With his knife pressing against a rock he cut off most of the wings and hackles. He tied the fly on and about a foot above it fastened a split shot.

I would have given odds of ten to one against that fly with those big Assinica brookies. But I said nothing. At least it would get his mind off the problems he would have to face when he returned to Boston.

I sat on the shore and smoked and watched. Jono went to the current's edge and cast a long line straight upstream. The current was strong, so he had to retrieve fast as the line moved down. When the leader was almost in front of him he quickly raised his rod tip. It whipped down and I knew he was on a fish. The loose line coiled in his hand started running out through the guides.

Those Assinica trout are powerful, and they do not quit easily if you use light tackle. This one moved into deep water and, with the current behind it, took out a hundred feet of line before Jono turned it and worked it slowly back. I weighed it in the net— five pounds exactly. I said, "Let's kill it. I want to see what's in its stomach."

"Nope!" Jono answered. "I know what's in its stomach— nymphs."

Fifteen minutes later with an identical fly trimmed and

fished in the same manner, I caught one and did kill it. Jono was right; its stomach bulged with small dark nymphs.

We each caught two more, and then, just before quitting time, Jono took his fourth, a beautiful lantern-jawed male with a deep-red belly that weighed six and three-quarters pounds. I said, "This one we kill, because I want to have it mounted for your Christmas present."

He finally, reluctantly, agreed to let me put a fish tie on it and fasten it to a tree. He said, "Let's see what happens tomorrow."

On the morrow we caught and released nine, all of them between four and five and a half pounds. It was one of the greatest days of my life. Now Jono was himself again and I knew that he would resolve his problems, as indeed he did, and that he would not have to do it in a state of depression.

When it was time to quit he said, "Dad, thanks for offering me the mounted trout. But really I would rather think of it here in the river."

He knelt on the ledge, drew the big trout in and took the plastic hook from its lower jaw. We watched it move slowly out from the shore, then with a flash of speed disappear.

Jono stood up and looked out at the big river. The water had taken on a golden hue from the setting sun and tall black spruce trees lined the far shore. The river gurgled as the current moved around boulders and past the ledges. Far off a whippoorwill cried like the sound of a tearing sheet. Jono drew in his breath and threw his shoulders back and said, "God! It is good to be alive and here."

❧❧❧ Lady in a Bar

Without an occasional drink there would not be much point to life, even for a fisherman who is so far ahead of non-fishermen to start with. So in the evening when the sun went down I stopped in at the Coldstream Bar in Coldstream, Scotland, and ordered a Scotch and soda from Mrs. Angletree, the hefty barmaid. "Make it a double," I said, "and easy on the soda." Then, being the only customer at the bar, I proceeded to tell Mrs. Angletree about the huge salmon that had swirled at my fly but hadn't taken.

Suddenly a girl appeared from the back of the room and sat down beside me. What a girl! How I had missed her I can't imagine. She would have made the reasonably experienced Hugh Heffner behave like a leaf in a hurricane. Tall, dark hair and dark eyes the size of saucers, followed downward by a tight sweater that did not even pretend to hide what was so generously stacked up beneath it, a small waist, and long beautiful legs, the tops of which disappeared into one of the shortest skirts in history.

She said, "Hello!" and I slopped half my drink over the bar.

"Mind if I join you, even if you are a fisherman? I hate fishing," she announced. "It's a cruel sport and a complete waste of time. Maggie, give me my special Scotch. And make mine a double too."

I gurgled out something that was supposed to sound like, "The drinks are on me." I wondered if I ought to tell her that I was thinking of giving up fishing for life, that I had really always hated it.

By the time we had finished our fourth round of doubles I had explained that the only reason I fished was that I loved to eat fish in spite of the torture of standing up to my hips in icewater hurling a mess of feathers at them. And then the awful strain of having to play the damned things.

"It must be horrible," she agreed, turning and smiling up at me. "Why don't you buy your fish in a market the way the rest of us do?"

I finally managed to pry my eyes off her bosom long enough to mumble something about market fish never being really fresh and about how Uncle Francis had almost died from ptomaine poisoning from eating a market fish he thought was fresh. And then there was my Great Aunt Eunice who did expire, and from eating a market salmon of all things.

"Let's have another round," she suggested. "I have never been so thirsty."

A few more rounds followed, and I was having some trouble telling the floor from the ceiling.

"Where were you on the Tweed?" she asked. "I'm a bird watcher and I know the Tweed well. I walk along it and look at the birds."

"Well, you know the bwidge— bridge, I mean. It hash an iron wailing and there ish a keough in a pashure, it seems to me I think."

She nodded her exquisite head, which was now beginning to spin around a bit. "Oh, yes, you must have been at the Border Maid. Lots of pheasants and grouse around there."

"O' course. I seen huneds, maybe tousand of 'em," I lied. "Well, there's an old willow– at's a twee– that hangs over the bank. Wight under dat willow is where he ish."

"Ugh!" she said. "You mean a fish?" She shuddered and I almost fell off my stool. "There are two swans that have a nest right above the pool. I love to watch them. The pen has been there for years, but the old cob died and now she has a new one. They're lovely birds. But you'd best not trouble the nest. Let's have another drink, a nightcap, shall we?"

I gripped the bar rail with both hands to try and keep the bar from sliding out of the taproom. "Yup!" I said. "Nudder one."

"And make them doubles," she added.

She thought she was sober, I decided. But she wasn't, or she wouldn't be spinning around like a top that way. You couldn't fool me. But anyway, she was mighty beautiful, even if she was always tilted. I tried looking at her with one eye closed, but that made her start to sail across the room.

"That's it," Mrs. Angletree announced. "You've both had a plenty." She shoved the umpteenth drinks toward us. "Finish them off. Time to close down."

How I got back to my room and up the stairs I fail to recall. But I do remember how I felt the next morning: as if a quarrying operation were going on inside my skull. I groaned and pulled up the blankets to shut out the light. My mouth tasted as though I had a gardener's mitten in it. I tried to go back to sleep but couldn't. Have you ever tried to sleep with someone hitting you on the top of the head with a hammer? I glanced at my watch and groaned. Ten of ten. And I had promised to meet my ghillie at the Border Maid at eight sharp.

Two Alka-Seltzer tablets, a cold shower, and black coffee, and I could walk about two feet in a reasonably straight line. I took off for the river in my rented car and my prayers were answered— I did not meet the Coldstream cop, who certainly would have thrown me into jail on a drunken-driving charge, or perhaps into the nearest garbage can.

At the river I located my ghillie, Binnie, sound asleep under the willow. I was giving serious thought to stretching out beside him when I heard a huge splash. Either that was a salmon the size of a porpoise or someone had fallen out of a tree into the river. And then I saw her.

The girl of the night before, fresh as a daisy, waders up to her ribs, and water almost to the tops of them, was playing a fish and playing it beautifully. The girl who hated to fish, the girl with my big salmon on . . .

"Hi!" she called. "I've had him on for twenty minutes. I think he's getting tired. You're here earlier than I expected."

Even with my pickled brains floating in alcohol I knew, somehow, that I had been had. "I thought you hated fishing," I snarled. "And for your information, I have leased this water and you are trespassing."

With her rod held high, her thumb expertly braking the reel, she said, "You made fishing sound so interesting I decided to try it. And I am not trespassing, I am fishing for trout. This river is open for trout fishing."

"Call that thing you have on a trout?" I shouted. "That's my salmon."

"It's just because I don't know anything about fishing," she explained. "I hooked him by mistake. I would love to give him to you, that is if I beach him, but unfortunately the rule of the river is that salmon caught by trout fishermen must be released or given to the pool's owner." She leaned forward, grabbed the tired salmon and expertly tailed it, dragged it ashore and hit it on the head with a rock. It must have weighed over thirty pounds, a very fine salmon, and a pretty rare one for the Tweed.

My ghillie was now awake. "Hunh!" he snorted. "The laird's not here and you know it, Miss Molly. So how are you going to give it to him? Aye, Miss Molly, there is no two ways to look at it, you are the Tweed's worst poacher and a thief into the bargain."

The salmon quivered and Molly hit it on the head again. She glanced at me. "Gawd!" she said. "You look awful." Then she picked up her fish and departed.

I never saw her again. But that afternoon when I stopped at the Coldstream Bar for a desperately needed pick-me-up Mrs. Angletree handed me a note. "Dear sir, here are five pounds, three shillings sixpence too much you paid for my drinks. The 'special' brand of Scotch I was drinking was made of tea. In war, love, and fishing just about everything is fair, but I don't want to cheat you on the drinks. Tight lines. Molly."

I sipped my whisky sour and gazed at the hefty barmaid. "So you were in on it all the time," I said accusingly.

"This drink and another you badly need are on the house," responded Mrs. Angletree. "And o' course I knew. Molly is my favorite niece and there isn't a finer fly fisherman the breadth of Scotland. Her grandfather, the Black Cat, occasionally descended to a spoon, but never Molly. As for you, a word to the wise should suffice. Americans are fine people, but they're given to talking too much. Yours is the third salmon from the

third American Molly has taken this year. And the season is only half gone. Others she'll be getting. That's for sure."

I groaned and swallowed my drink. And from that day to this I have never spoken of a big fish, at least not until it was landed or given up for good.

ﻬﻬﻬThe Black Cat

Molly had come by her poaching naturally, because her grandfather, known as the Black Cat, was certainly the Tweed's finest all-time poacher, if not all of Scotland's. And this is saying a good deal, for the two or three dozen ghillies who have lived on the Tweed's banks for twenty years or more know a thing or two themselves about how to capture the salmon, grouse, and pheasants illegally in all seasons of the year.

The Black Cat, under the law that permits anyone to fish any part of the Tweed for trout, had unquestionably put more salmon down on ice than any owner of riparian rights, plus all the guests the best of them had allowed to fish.

Berwick's bailiff had been after the Black Cat for fifteen years, indeed since he had first quit being a gardener and

donned his badge, but the story was always the same: "Yes, he was here, and a fine salmon he was carrying, but he left five minutes ago." Enough to drive a bailiff crazy. And the Black Cat almost did.

But then finally came the day when the bailiff nailed the Black Cat dead to rights. He, the bailiff, had been breaking in a young assistant, showing him how to sneak along the river's bank so you came upon your poacher without being seen. Around a bend in the river they went and there was the Black Cat, right out in the middle of the stream fishing a great greenheart rod with a large salmon fly. There would be no sad tale of being after trout this time, not when the judge beheld that rod and fly. The bailiff licked his lips. "Come on," he whispered. "We got him. There will be no escapin' this time."

The bailiff charged out onto the shore, the young assistant bailiff at his heels. "Come in, mon, yer under arrest," he shouted.

The Black Cat, a man of six feet four and two hundred and twenty pounds of bone and muscle, turned his head and glanced at the old bailiff, a man of medium height, and the boy beside him. Then he turned his back on them and cast again.

A salmon rose and he hooked it.

"And now you have a salmon. And I have this young witness to swear to it. Six months behind the bars is what yer goin' to get." The bailiff was hopping up and down with glee. "Come in now and don't argue."

The Black Cat ignored him and played the fish.

"Come in or I'm comin' in after ye," yelled the bailiff.

The Black Cat caught the salmon and banged it on the head with his priest, a large priest designed for salmon only. He ran a cord through the gill and mouth, fastened the salmon to his belt, took two steps downstream, and started fishing again.

The bailiff turned to his assistant, a husky boy in his early twenties. "Roger, go on and bring him ashore. He's under arrest. Here, take this billy. Hit him if needs be."

The Black Cat kept on fishing. If he was aware of the existence of the two wardens he didn't show it.

Roger stepped into the river and waded out. The Black Cat ignored him until he was four feet away. Then he stopped fishing, suddenly raised a huge knee above the surface, and brought the heavy greenheart rod down on it, breaking it off a few feet above the reel. He grabbed the shattered end in one hand and, quick as a cat, swung it in an arc and landed the heavy butt with the salmon reel above it on the young bailiff's head. Then he stood there and watched the unconscious young man float downstream toward the sea.

The old bailiff, seething mad, danced a jig of anger on the shore. He had two choices now, one to arrest the Black Cat and take him in, the other to run downstream and save his assistant before he drowned. He chose the latter course. After all, the town cop could bring the poacher in. His own testimony and Roger's would suffice. He ran downstream and out into the water.

The Black Cat waded ashore, threw the salmon over his back, stopped by a bush, and took the hand of five-year-old Molly, who, God bless her, hadn't moved a muscle. A fine woman and a splendid poacher she was going to be.

An hour later the bailiff, accompanied by an assistant with a large lump on his head, plus the uniformed town cop, found the Black Cat in a local pub, a bottle of beer beside him. On his knee sat his exquisite little granddaughter, stolidly sucking her thumb as she viewed the world through enormous irresistible eyes. There was a loud plopping sound, like a champagne cork leaving the bottle, as she withdrew her thumb and announced, "Granddaddy's been here all afternoon."

"Granddaddy's going to jail," shouted the bailiff. He turned to the cop. "Arrest the mon. He's the one. An hour ago I found him salmon fishin' and then the bloody rascal resisted arrest."

There were seventeen Scotchmen in the bar, drinking beer and playing darts. All seventeen now backed Molly up and announced they were ready to go to court and swear the Black Cat had been there the last three hours at least. Not a doubt about it.

The policeman stopped fingering his truncheon and scratched his head.

The Black Cat sighed sadly and looked at the boiling bailiff. "It must have been someone else," he said. "Don't feel bad. We all make mistakes." He ordered a round of beer for the two bailiffs and the cop.

And on the following day the head bailiff turned in his badge and went back to mowing lawns.

ᕭᕭᕭ Paddy O'Hara

The guide Paddy O'Hara is not to be found in Boston or Dublin, where O'Haras, O'Briens, and Murphys are thicker than flies on a dead hog, but, of all places, in northern Ontario. And even in Ontario he's hard to come by. Promises, yes; Paddy will promise you anything, but delivery . . . Well, I guess you need the luck of the Irish, and not being Irish I didn't have it.

Fly casters, you never saw Paddy's equal from Greenland to Tierra del Fuego. Experts, all please to one side and make room for Paddy O'Hara, five feet five inches of red-headed Irishman with a glass tarpon rod, a heavy shooting-head line, and two hundred yards of nylon backing. Fly casts of a hundred and forty feet, nothing to it. That little man with the big rod is one of Canada's finest trout fishermen, and to hear him tell it in his own modest manner, the world's all-time greatest, but still a man with a ten-and-a-half-pound brook trout to his credit (that one, so help me, is the truth, because the fish, very badly stuffed with the straw coming out of it, hangs on a wall of a fishing club with its exact weight and Paddy's name beneath it), four times the champion lake-trout fisherman of the country, and also, and not to be sneezed at either, the former skeet champion of Canada. A superb wing shot, a man with a lovely wife and fourteen kids at last count, a naturalist who knows every bird, fish, beast, and blade of grass by its Latin name, and, according to him, has caught so many brookies of over eight pounds you get the idea that for him an average day on the river yields up from forty to fifty pounds of trout. That is the red-headed Paddy O'Hara of North Bay. But he, in spite of his skills, is given to gilding the lily a bit when it comes to fish.

There was the time when he and I were guiding for four of his cash customers near Sturgeon Falls. As his idea of guiding is to let the cash customers fend for themselves, fall in the river and drown if they must while he goes forth and catches the fish, on this particular afternoon he was busy working a wet fly downstream. I was sitting with a bush at my back watching a very nice lady from Indianapolis, whom I had been coaching, fish a pool upstream. Below me was Paddy, and I could see his every move, including the catching of one pretty small trout which he banged on the head and put in his creel.

Finally the lady gave up and walked back to the station wagon. I waited until Paddy finally quit, then headed back at the same time. We got there right together. "What luck?" he asked. There was the usual silence from the paying guests, meaning none of them had caught a thing. So Paddy produced his trout, in his customary casual manner, and slapped it down on the hood of the car, a fish of about two pounds. "Got six, one of seven or eight pounds. Put them all back, then I re-membered I promised Em a trout so I kept this little thing."

The four hundred-dollar-a-day customers, now, as usual, re-duced to ashes, silently took their places in the station wagon.

"I was on the bank just above you," I announced. "I could see your every move. I will say you were casting a very long line."

"Were you there?" Paddy asked, in tones that implied a most unhappy end for me if I carried the conversation further.

I am fond of Paddy, though there have been numerous occa-sions when I would have been glad to wring his neck, so I let him get away with it. After all, the customers were his; I was just guiding for fun and to learn the rivers in that area.

Paddy has a great deal to him that is most commendable. The first time I met him was in the company of the late Tony Jensen, reported to be the richest U. S. citizen operating north of the border. Anyway, Tony was plenty rich and always in with whoever occupied the saddle at the moment from the Prime Minister down the ladder. That takes more than a little skill in Canada, with the powerful French Canadians contin-ually trying to harpoon everyone west of Montreal. Tony was very smart and a hard worker. But when he relaxed he did it with a vengeance. And when he fished, which he claimed to love, he also relaxed, right to the bottom of one bottle after another.

There were eight of us in the party. But other than Tony the only ones I remember were Paddy and an extremely at-tractive blond lady from Boston named Kitty Cabot. I guess that the best reason for remembering Paddy and Kitty was that they and I were the only three members of the party who were not completely boiled before the fishing even started.

One of Tony's hired hands had erected a tent on the river's

edge where we could escape a sun that was hot enough to fry eggs, even that far north. In the center of the tent was a big old-fashioned wash tub full of ice, and around the tub were enough bottles of Canadian Club, Scotch, bourbon, and gin to have put a dozen people under the table.

"I am going fishing," announced Paddy in some disgust.

I said that I would come along and the lovely Boston blonde said that she would too. Tony and his cronies assured us that they would be along— just as soon as they had one more. Apparently one led to another, because we never saw any of them on the river.

So Paddy, the Boston blonde, and I went pike fishing, and the blonde and I tried our hands at a way of fishing that Paddy had invented.

The river was full of weeds two or three feet in length, in which a fly or lure would be lost immediately. The problem, which Paddy had solved, was to bring the pike up out of the weeds into the clear water above, where you would have at least a fighting chance of hooking him. We fished with spinning rods. Paddy tied on a cork float at the end of the line and another float four feet up the line. Then he tied four hooks with six-inch gut leaders between the floats and baited these with small pieces of fish. He explained that you cast this paraphernalia out into the middle of the river, then wound in until the corks were the maximum distance apart and you knew your hooks were not tangled together. "And you wait," he said. "You will see the pike swirl around your baits. When one of the corks moves, strike, quick."

Sounds easy. All I can say is, try it. I caught one pike, Kitty Cabot none, while Paddy got six.

With the sixth Paddy suggested that we get out of the sun, which now was directly overhead in a cloudless windless sky and as hot as if we had been astride the equator. "It's time for lunch," he said. "Take a deep breath of fresh air before diving back into the bar."

Back in the tent we found two English Canadians, two French Canadians, and Tony Jensen in various states of inebriation.

"We're going fishing shortly," babbled the U. S.'s richest Canadian operator. "Jus' one more drink. Cep' for him, he's passed out."

We ate our sandwiches and the Boston blonde said, "The fumes in this place would put a longshoreman under. Let's go fishing before we all pass out too."

Paddy swallowed his third Coke and said, "Better wait till the sun goes down a bit. Miss Cabot looks a little burned to me. Or if you are going to fish I suggest you go upstream about a mile to where there is a big shade tree at the edge of a good pool."

Kitty Cabot surveyed the surrounding drunks and said, "Good. I'm all for it— the shade tree, I mean."

I announced that I would accompany her, and Paddy said that he would go downstream in the other direction.

Kitty and I came to a tight wire cattle fence about four feet high with a strand of barbed wire along the top. I climbed it first, then helped her over. Getting her to the other side was not exactly easy.

We never made it to the shade tree, a good mile from the booze tent. When we were nearly there Kitty moaned, pressed a hand against her brow, and collapsed on the ground, out like a light. Too much sun. I covered her head with my hat— she had none— and ran back to the tent for help. But Paddy had gone and the others couldn't even help themselves. I have a slightly crippled left arm, and at that time I was nearing sixty. How I made the trip back to the fence with that female over my shoulder I will never know. But I finally got her to the fence, and that stymied me. There was just one thing to do and I did it. I dumped her over like a sack of wheat. Happily she landed tail first.

I dragged her into the tent.

"She dead?" inquired one of the occupants. "Les drink to her."

"Should never take a woman fishing," said Tony. "Even if her father ish one o' my besh frens."

"Shut up and make room," was my comment. I stretched her out between the two passed-out French Canadians and put ice on her brow and the back of her neck. "Tony, I don't care how drunk you are. Go get Paddy. This girl is in bad shape."

"No ushe. She's dead," said Tony. "Wanna drink?"

It was no use trying to get something out of Tony. I kept putting fresh ice on her brow, temples, and neck. At the end of ten minutes she moaned and put her hand toward her brow, then dropped it. She was as white as a ceiling. I reached over and took the glass out of Tony's hand and told him, in unprintable words, what I thought of him. Then he took over the ice job and I went after Paddy.

With Paddy driving his truck down a country dirt road at seventy miles an hour, we got her to a hospital, one, incidentally, that Tony had given to northern Ontario in one of his soberer moments. Forty-eight hours later she emerged, very pale around the gills, and insisting that it was the alcoholic fumes that had put her under and not the sun. Paddy and I took her out to dinner. So, in spite of his manifold failings, I have loved Paddy ever since. And heaven knows that Paddy is not the first fisherman to exaggerate a bit. Even I have been known to do it now and then, though not nearly as often as my friends claim.

After that Paddy and I corresponded a lot, and he wrote mouth-watering tales of all the huge fish he was catching in the rivers around Lake Nepessing. He promised that we would fish every day together and I ought to get at least ten brook trout in the eight-pound class, indeed probably a few more than that. Eight pounds! Ten of them! The biggest brookie I have ever caught was one that weighed just six and a half.

So the answer to all the letters was that my wife and I rented a camp, sight unseen, and spent two months in North Bay. It was the worst summer on record, claimed the town's eldest inhabitants. It was awful— rain, snow, hurricane winds, the rivers all in spate, day after day of looking out of our leaky living-room window to the mountainous white crested waves on the lake. Enough to cause the president of the Women's Christian Temperance Union to hit the bottle.

And the fishing? Tomorrow Paddy would go. Today an emergency had arisen and he couldn't make it. Two and a half weeks of this and I threw in the sponge, got out a road map, and went fishing on my own. I selected the South River, then a famous brook-trout stream. It was a raging torrent a yard over the banks and a hundred yards wide, and I cast into the teeth of a gale. On the third day of freezing to death and hauling trout flies out of the bushes that lined the banks, I caught a three-pounder. Life is too short, I decided. Better to stay home and watch the roof leak, keep Sylvia company, and read a book, or swat the bugs coming up out of the kitchen drain.

That evening the elusive Paddy stopped by for a drink. "No, no," he said, "there are no real fish there where you've been. You were on the wrong part of the river. Tomorrow I will show you."

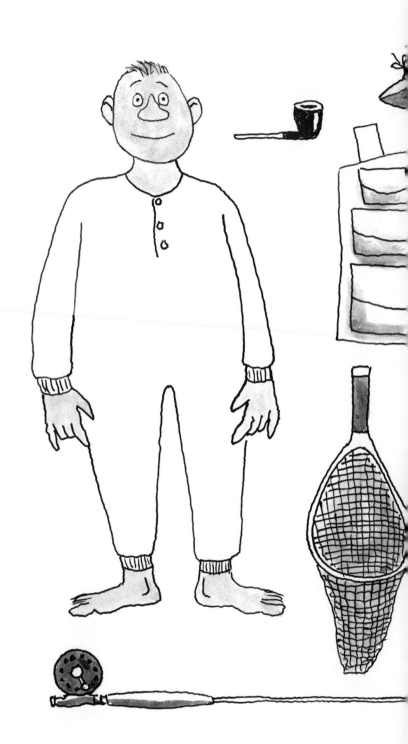

I am sure that Paddy saw Sylvia and me exchange glances. Paddy and his damned tomorrows . . . It didn't bother him a bit. "Tomorrow," he said, "the British ambassador wants to fish and I am guiding for him. No reason for you not to come along. Presumably he doesn't know how to fish— none of my paying customers ever do— but you and I ought to get some trout. Steak for lunch. Better come."

"Count me in," I said, assuming at the last minute that the trip would be called off and Paddy would be in Boston, Montreal, or Dallas.

"I want to get an early start, so let's meet at my place at eight," added Paddy.

At eight the next morning the British ambassador and I were there. He was a pleasant chap, a foreign diplomat of the old school who had been around a long time and obviously knew the foreign-service ropes.

On the dot of eleven Paddy showed up and said, "Let's get going," as if his nibs and I had been holding up the parade for much too long a time.

Ten miles out of town, we turned off the paved road, right by the river, drove a few rods down a dirt road, and came to a locked farm gate. Paddy looked in all his pockets. He had forgotten the key. Happily a farm hand turned up who had one and who also knew that Paddy had rights to fish the farm, so we did not lose another hour while Paddy went home, presumably to learn that he had left the key in Ottawa.

While Paddy and I gathered wood and built a fire the ambassador fished. He was not a long-line fisherman, but he worked the edges of the wide flooded river and did it well, with no luck. A half-hour later we dined on reasonably tough steak (Paddy was a great bargain shopper) that had been dropped in the ashes twice— no problem, Paddy wiped most of the ashes off on the seat of his pants. With it we had bread that we tore off the long roll with our hands because somehow the knife had been forgotten, and a bottle of pretty awful U. S. red wine. After all, what do you expect for a hundred bucks a day? Salad? We got in Paddy's pickup and drove a few miles through cow pastures to a stream Paddy guaranteed was loaded with trout of over eight pounds, not to mention the pike of over twenty-five.

By the end of the afternoon the ambassador and I had each taken a brookie of around two and a half pounds and Paddy had the customary tale of one over nine pounds that finally got away. It had been a nice day, and the ambassador and I were content. All the way back to town Paddy rattled on about huge trout he had caught or lost, and the stories, of which we didn't believe a word, rolled over us like rain dripping over a couple of frogs.

That evening Paddy again stopped by. Alas, he had a problem. His fishing club was having an outing and a contest for the biggest fish. As a very special favor would I mind guiding for the ambassador? No, I didn't mind, but I also did not have the faintest idea of where to take him to wade and fish.

That, explained Paddy, was easy. If I had a paper and pencil he would draw me a map. And if we did not bring home at least one brookie of over seven pounds he would be glad to eat the map. Why, just the last time he was there . . . He was off again on those ten-pounders that apparently lurked in every pool of the stream. And speaking of eating things, he said, though no one had been speaking of eating anything, he would have sandwiches prepared for our lunch because on the morrow he had asked the ambassador to dinner and was going to give him the best steak in Canada.

Sylvia told him not to worry, she would prepare lunch. She

knew as well as I did that if Paddy was going into a fishing contest he would never remember the bread, let alone the stuff that went in between.

The ambassador and I had a fine day, and he, just before quitting time, caught a twenty-one-pound pike. We cast, as usual, into a gale. Apparently to be a fisherman one has to put up with everything, and we did just that. At least the lunch Sylvia provided almost made up for it— tender broilers that I cooked under a large tree that kept the rain off us, fresh peas, a delicious salad, fried potatoes, melon, a bottle of good French white wine, and tea, not in bags but cooked in a pot in deference to the land the Englishman came from. Then, when he had the pike on, he fell in the river. He swam ashore, his rod still held high, and finally worked the big pike in close enough for me to grab it and toss it up on shore. I told him I would build a fire and he could start by putting on my sweater. He shook his head, lay down on his back, and raised his feet so that gallons of water could run out of his waders. "Jolly fine pike," he said. "Biggest one I've ever caught. Know how to skin a fish for mounting?"

I nodded. "I'll do it at home. Temperature is in the forties. Let's get you out of here before you freeze to death."

At our camp I loaned him dry clothes and gave him a good stiff slug of Scotch. "Sure you know how to prepare that fish for the taxidermist?" he asked.

I reassured him and with a last admiring glance at the pike we took off for Paddy's. Paddy arrived an hour late with a story of how he had just missed, by a hair mind you, getting the largest fish. Finally the ambassador managed to tell him about his pike.

"Twenty-one pounds," Paddy said. "A little one. I have caught a number there of over thirty pounds. Once I hooked into one I am sure was over forty . . ." And Paddy was off again.

As I departed the ambassador winked and said, "Don't forget to skin that little pike of mine. I want to show how small they come."

Sometime later I learned that while Paddy was telling the ambassador about all the enormous pike he'd caught his mongrel managed to sneak the steak off the kitchen table and depart into the bush, so His Excellency wound up eating bread and butter.

The next day the ambassador headed south to Ottawa and back to work, and Paddy asked me if I would take another customer, this one from Troy, New York. It seems the fishing contest was to be continued. Anyway, the young man from Troy was a very nice chap. I guided for him three days— that fishing contest went on and on— and our total take was one three-pound trout I caught and a terrible cold in the head for the cash customer. He, poor guy, never caught a trout in Ontario, but I am happy to learn from a recent letter that next summer he is going back to fish with Paddy again. There is something about trout fishing in Canada that gets into the blood, or into the brain (this last on the assumption that fishermen have one), or perhaps it gets into both.

During our second month in North Bay everything changed for the better. I ran across a very nice boy up there on his honeymoon who had a pickup truck, a boat, and an outboard engine. His bride . . . ah, yes, she was working in a tobacco shop to keep from being bored to death while her husband fished seven days a week from early breakfast to a very late dinner. So for a month I caught trout, lakers, and pike, lots of them, mostly casting along the shores of small lakes. But no big ones. The big ones started the day I left, when Johnny took someone out who had never fished before in his life. Trolling with a spoon, he nailed a seven-and-a-half-pound brookie. Such is life, and doubtless that is one of the reasons we keep on going back.

Our next trip was with four old friends whom I had persuaded to come north— again the monster trout saga— and Paddy was our guide. We stayed at an inn in Sturgeon Falls and rose early to breakfast each morning and be all set for Paddy by eight sharp. At about nine-thirty Paddy and the pickup would arrive and generally by quarter after ten we would be off for a fifty- or sixty-mile drive over the most god-awful roads in Canada. They curved around like a coiled rattler and were surfaced with deep mud. Every time a car passed we went through a spray of goo that camouflaged our car till it would have made an excellent duck blind.

Finally we reached a swollen river with water spread out on both sides twenty feet from the banks. "That pool. See that pool right there," said Paddy. "Caught a nine-pounder there a couple of weeks ago. Jane, you try it. There is one over ten pounds there. Missed him a few days ago."

Jane was a lady in her early fifties from Buffalo who couldn't cast her way out of a paper bag. A twenty-foot cast for her was doing fine. But like the other customers she adored Ontario, the trails, the dark-green hills, the streams and lakes that were everywhere, the beaver swimming the ponds or slapping their tails and diving, the occasional moose thigh-deep in the water to escape the flies, a black bear, and once a timberwolf. We heard the wolf howl far away, and Paddy imitated the cry perfectly. Five seconds later back came an answer. Then Paddy again. Back and forth they howled. We all crouched down behind a dead tree at the edge of a clearing and a few minutes later the wolf trotted into full view, sniffed the air, caught our scent, and departed on the run. We saw a great many Canada geese, swimming with their young or flying overhead in long jagged V's, the lonely sound of their honking floating down from the sky, and once in a while a small house miles removed from its nearest neighbor or an old abandoned lumber camp. A million miles from New York or Chicago; it was not hard to love northern Ontario, unimproved by man, just about the way God had left it.

Well, the fiftyish Jane, a complete plumber with a fly rod, fished that pool while nearby Sylvia did a landscape painting, and the rest of us worked other stretches and Paddy the guide took off for parts unknown.

At one o'clock we gathered by the car for a picnic lunch. As usual Paddy stalked up and slapped down a medium-sized trout on the car's hood, and as usual he had hooked and lost one a yard long.

Before he could ask his usual question, in that awful weather and high water, damn well knowing the answer, "What luck did the rest of you have?" Jane beat him to the punch and inquired, "Is nine pounds a pretty good brookie?"

Paddy was off on just how good a nine-pounder is and what an incredible amount of skill it takes to catch one. Just not for the average fisherman, he explained. Why, to tell us the truth . . . And he was down the track full tilt on how such trout are very very seldom taken except by a handful of top fly fishermen, one of whom, by chance, happened to be himself.

"If a nine-pounder is that hard to take, what about one weighing nine and a half pounds?" asked Jane sweetly.

Paddy is not dumb. He looked at her, hard. Something was up and he knew it. "A nine-and-a-half-pounder?" he asked suspiciously.

She smiled and pointed. "Over there, behind the tree. You

forgot to leave a net with me so Sylvia landed it by hand."

First we all looked at the beautiful, enormous, lantern-jawed male brookie (the largest brookie killed in North America in three years), then all of us but Paddy bombarded Jane with questions. Paddy was about as deflated as a toy balloon that has just encountered a lighted match. But over the picnic wine he made a feeble comeback. "Don't you remember," he said, "I lost one about that size right in this pool a while back. That's the same fish, all right."

Someone sniggered.

Jane picked the big trout up, said nothing, but swaggered up to the car and slammed it down on the hood. "How'd the rest of you do?" she asked.

And for the next four days, until the trip ended, Paddy stopped telling about all the huge trout he had lost, and he stopped slapping dead trout down on the car before asking the others how they had fared. If he caught any— and he is a fine fisherman, so he probably did— they were returned to the water to grow.

All that was a year ago. This morning, back home in Connecticut, I received a letter from him about a new stretch of water he has discovered where the brookies grow to enormous size. In fact he is sure that someone is going to take a fifteen-pounder from that water and set a new world's record. And if I will come north he will put off guiding and we'll fish together every day.

Sylvia says that I'm nuts, but she has agreed to come along with me for one more try.

✐✐✐ Jill

Jill Wcford is petite, beautiful, genteel, and equipped with the pre-Civil War charm that Hollywood has been unsuccessfully trying to emulate since movies were invented. I had asked Jill and her husband, R. L., to join Sylvia and me for a week's fishing at the St. Bernard Club in Quebec, and they had accepted.

Down home in Gladiola, Mississippi, Jill was faced with a problem. She had never cast a fly in her life, and R. L., who knew how, was too busy with his cotton crop to teach her. He wrote to Orvis and outfitted her with rod, reel, line, flies, leaders, et cetera. And with a picture book on how to cast.

Jill went to work beneath the cottonwoods on their spacious lawn. At the end of a week and seven hours of practice, Jill, a young lady of far above average intelligence, had proved that you can learn fly casting from a book. She could handle fifty feet of line and leader credibly.

Our camp at the St. Bernard Club was on Sorcier, a ten-mile-long lake that, prior to being grabbed by the Province of Quebec, offered some of the world's finest landlocked-salmon fishing. But the first morning in camp hardly looked inviting. It was cold, *very* cold, and raw. Dark storm clouds raced out of the northeast, and the wind churned up the lake. Sylvia said, "I suggest we troll up to the trail to the Lakes Simones, catch some trout and have lunch up there, then troll home."

So that's what we did. Jill's book on fly fishing had contained nothing on trolling, but she now received a lesson in this subject, delivered in French Canadian patois— of which she understood not a word— by her elderly guide, who still boasted two of his own teeth, giving him two more than most Quebec guides can claim. So Sylvia's guide paddled close to Jill's canoe while Sylvia instructed Jill. R. L. and I cast close along the shores, leaving the ladies to fend for themselves. Not a salmon was taken by anyone.

When we all beached our canoes a few miles from camp to hit the mile uphill trail to the two Simones, Jill, beautifully garbed as always, and warmly enough for some winter exploration work in Greenland, still looked thoroughly frozen. And there were occasional snow flurries in the air.

"Mah, it's cold," she said in her mellifluous Mississippi accent.

Since ladies all require more organizing time than men, R. L. and I marched up the trail behind our guides, who had our canoes on their shoulders. When we reached the first Simone I suggested we paddle across it, wallow through a hundred feet of mud and water to the second pond, and leave the first for the ladies. I said, "Not as many trout in the second, but generally they are quite a bit larger."

So the rest of the tale about Jill is secondhand, told me by

Sylvia. When she and Jill reached the first pond she suggested to Jill that she go fishing. She said, "I want to get the luncheon organized and make sure the guides don't drink up all the cocktails before we start."

Now Jill was on her own, for the first casting experience since her practice on the Mississippi lawn of Weford Hall. Not being used to Canadian weather— she had never been north of New York City before— she fished with her heavy knitted gloves on. Not an easy task for a Lee Wulff, even less easy for a Southern belle in search of her first trout.

"Ah have one," she called. And indeed she did.

Sylvia left the fire and stood on the shore to watch. Jill's trout was a nice one, about twelve inches long, six inches more than Jill was equipped to handle.

The book on casting had restricted itself to just that. The playing of a fish presumably was for a later volume. Jill was quickly a mess of snarled line and ponderous gloves. She took the finger of one glove between her teeth and pulled it off and dropped it— in the pond. She tried to rescue the glove and si-multaneously the trout made a run for the pond's center. By the time its run stopped, the glove had sunk to the bottom and Jill had pulled off her other glove.

Her two-toothed guide, bellowing instructions in patois, was of no assistance. Sylvia decided not to add to the con-fusion. At this point Jill hit on a method, a new one but her own. She grabbed the line in her teeth, pulled the trout in a bit by raising her tip, then let the tip down, drew in the slack gained with her hand and took a fresh bite. About fifteen bites brought the trout alongside and the guide netted it.

Sylvia returned to the fire and to arranging the lunch. Half an hour later it started to snow, hard. Jill, shivering from head to toe, joined her. She held out her hands to the flames, wet and red from the cold. She had caught six trout, a good enough catch for a male employing his reel, or retrieving and playing the fish by hand, superb for a Southern lady employing her teeth.

The snowflakes drifted down and the wind howled through the trees. Jill shivered again. "Sylvia," she said, "how fah is it to the Noth Pole?"

Sylvia said she was tempted to point to the far end of the pond and answer that it was just over that hill.

But her plans were interrupted. At that point R. L. and I returned, without a single fish.

Sylvia broke out laughing. "After lunch why don't you two take a lesson from Jill? You need to stop using your hands and learn to fish with your teeth. I'm sure you'd both do better."

To the best of my knowledge Jill has never trout-fished since. With her record she doesn't need to.

⌘⌘⌘ Upper Region of the Strong Ones

Trout in Lebanon, that pocket-sized country at the far end of the Mediterranean where girls lie on the beaches in their bikinis nine months out of the year and palm trees grow along the shore?

"Ah, but yes, in the mountains and the Beqaa Valley," Sadek explained. "Every year there are rainbows caught of twelve pounds, and browns up to seven."

I had been in the country four months and no one had even mentioned trout until this moment. To make matters worse, ten days earlier I had broken my arm and was wearing a cast and sling. My ribs had been banged up too, so taking a deep breath was pure agony. But if there was really trout fishing in Lebanon . . .

"Unfortunately this is not the best time of year," continued Sadek. "September, that is when you should be here. Then the rivers are low and you can wade upstream and fish the dry fly."

Since I was leaving for home in two weeks it was now or never. The next day Sylvia and I lunched with Sadek Tabbara and a fishing friend of his, Jacques Mahfoud, a heavy-set, silent young mechanical engineer. The forty-three-year-old Sadek is one of the Middle East's outstanding architects, whom I had met in conjunction with my work as a consultant to the Lebanese government. He is a cheerful smallish man who bounces through life like a squash ball.

These two men told us of fishing in the Litani, Abu Ali, Ibrahim, Jessine, Barouk, Nabaa Rouess, and Anjar rivers, and in Qaraoun Lake. Suddenly Jacques' face lit up. "The Helm Valley! We will go to the Abu Ali. It is a beautiful river in the desert. And I am sure you will be the *first* Americans ever to fish it."

The following Saturday, Sadek, Jacques, Sylvia, and I took off at six in the morning and raced through the narrow winding streets of Beirut at fifty miles an hour with Jacques, a magnificent driver, at the wheel of his souped-up car. When we left Beirut the speedometer moved up to seventy-five as we climbed into a long pass with steep snow-covered slopes on either side, tore down the far slope, and moved north into a broad valley.

Fifty miles out of Beirut we saw the towering columns of Baalbek, one of the finest Roman ruins in the world. Then we went off the tourist track and the road was full of washouts and holes. Here the only traffic was a man on a tiny donkey, or one walking in front of a laden camel, or a flock of sheep or goats with a woman tending them. Once we roared through a village of houses that must have been very much like those in the time of Christ, and we began to feel the loneliness and the isolation of the desert.

Sylvia said, "Tell us about the river we are going to fish, Sadek."

"The Abu Ali," exclaimed Sadek. "I do not think there can be another river like it anywhere. There is nothing but desert and this river that gushes out between rocks in a desert gorge. Where the water comes from no one knows, but it must be from very far away. Someplace up in the mountains that no one has ever found, the water from melting snows must go underground, travel for miles beneath the surface, and finally burst out in this one place to start the river down through Lebanon and Syria to the sea."

"What are the people like in that area?" Sylvia asked.

"They are lovely," said Sadek enthusiastically. "They are bandits."

"They are what?" cried Sylvia.

"Bandits," Sadek replied. "All very nice people, but most of the men are wanted by the police. You probably will not see any of them. They leave the villages early and do not come back until night. You only will see the women and children and two or three of the older boys who do not yet own guns. Most of the women have never been ten kilometers from their villages. The men often go to neighboring villages to see their friends, but the women and children are always left at home."

Sylvia sighed. "What a lonely life for a woman."

"But they do not mind. You see, they do not know any other life. Ah yes, there is one little thing before I forget. If you do see one of the older men he will be armed and you must not take his picture. It is because most of the men in the area are wanted for murder or some other thing, and so they are afraid to have their pictures taken."

Before either of us could comment on this, Jacques braked the car and we stopped in front of a roadblock of cement columns with a heavy steel bar between them. Two soldiers stepped out of a guardhouse, a sergeant who wore an automatic and a private who had a rifle cradled in his arm.

Jacques turned to me. "Do you have your passport?"

I handed it to him. Sylvia said, "Oh, dear, I forgot mine. I didn't know that we were going to have to cross the border into Syria."

"No, we are not crossing the border," Sadek told her. "You see sometimes there is lots of trouble when the Dandache and the Jaafirah tribes start fighting each other, so now the army has sealed them off and they check everyone who comes in or goes out. And then there is the hashish. Look! Just over there you see those little villages way back at the edge of the mountain. Those are the villages of the people who grow hashish. It is all around there for several miles. The army tries to stop them from smuggling it out, and to stop people from smuggling arms in and selling them to the bandits. That is why we need our passports, and they will search our car. But you do not need yours, Sylvia, because you are a woman."

The soldiers came toward us, the one with the rifle a few steps behind, backing up the sergeant. They looked as if they knew that we were not to be trusted. The sergeant took the passports, studied the photographs and compared them with our faces. He gave a passing glance at Sylvia and went into the guardhouse, the passports in his hand. The other soldier remained there, watching us. When the sergeant returned, he made Jacques get out and open the trunk. Finally they returned our passports and dropped the heavy steel bar to the ground so we could be on our way.

I said, "They really behaved as if they were expecting trouble."

Sadek lit a cigarette. "They are. They are afraid. The bandits have killed a lot of them. Once the army built a barracks overlooking Hermel, the largest town up here, and they kept nearly a hundred men there. But every night the bandits cut their wires and their water pipe, and the soldiers could never catch them. When they went out to repair the wires or the pipe the bandits shot them. So they gave up their camp and moved here. Now they get along pretty well, just so long as they do not make too much trouble for the bandits. It really works very well. The army protects them from the police. You see, in Lebanon every time a new baby is born the father has to pay the government a tax of five pounds. That is much money for these people. So now the army pays the tax and tries to keep the police out of the valley."

"I thought bandits were supposed to hold people up and rob them," Sylvia said.

"But it is as I told you. They do not bother their friends because they know that their friends will never harm them. Killing men in the other tribe, that is a very different matter; the two tribes have been doing that longer than anyone can remember. They themselves do not know when it started. And when someone who is wanted flees to this valley he must join one tribe or the other."

"But I still don't see why the army can't stop all this," I said.

Sadek shook his head. "The only way they could stop it would be to kill all the men on one side. No one wants to do that. So they try to keep them all here in this area and leave them alone— that is, unless a very big fight gets started, as one did three years ago. The last big fight was on a mountain, with hundreds of tribesmen on each side. First the army tried to break it up with soldiers, but that did not work because both sides stopped fighting each other and shot at the soldiers. Then they brought up tanks, but the mountain was too steep for them. Finally they stopped it by flying planes over and dropping rockets between the two sides. The bandits ran away from the rockets and the fight ended."

Sylvia looked at me. "What a lovely place to take your wife on a picnic," she remarked. "Sadek, how do these fights get started?"

Sadek said, "Mostly because of stealing goats, sheep, and women from the other tribe."

"Women!" Sylvia exclaimed.

Sadek nodded. "Yes. Many women are stolen every year. You see, the women tend the flocks. And if a woman is young and pretty and wanders too far into the desert, one of the bandits on the other side may capture her and take her home as an extra wife. This makes the woman's first husband very mad, so he feels he has to kill someone to get even. And then the killing goes back and forth until a war gets started or until the two sides get sick of it."

"But what is to keep the woman from going home to her own tribe?" I asked. "You say the men are away all day."

Sadek said, "The other women and boys not old enough to own guns watch her. If she tries to run away she is tied up. After a while she gets tired of it and is happy with her new husband. Then they let her tend the flocks alone. Everything would work out all right except for the husbands' feeling they have to kill someone."

During a further explanation of the provocative traits possessed by goats, sheep, and women belonging to opposing tribesmen, the barren desert was interrupted by long gently sloping brown fields with tiny villages in the distance. Jacques said that these were the fields of hashish that we had seen from the army post, and that they would soon be green with a new crop. He explained that after the crop is processed it is put into small tins and smuggled into Syria, and from there into Egypt, where it is distributed to the world's markets.

"Of course it is illegal," said Sadek. "But there is no way to stop it. Every little village has a lookout on guard, so if the police or the army go there they will find no one. They go into the mountains and hide."

"Why doesn't the army burn the fields?" I asked.

Sadek spread his hands in a gesture of hopelessness. "They can't do that. It is the only way the bandits have to earn their living."

Jacques slowed down and then took off straight across the desert. Soon we reached the top of a rise and looked down on a cluster of five small sand-colored buildings of stone and adobe. As we drove down into the village Sadek told us that it was called Ras el Assis, which means "The Upper Region of the Strong Ones." Each house had a curtained opening and wooden shutters that could be closed. There was no glass. The village stood on a point of land overlooking a deep gorge slashed across the face of the desert. It was a wild, forbidding spot. One could easily imagine killers living there.

A pack of tawny-colored beasts the size of German shepherds rushed at the parked car, growling and snapping and jumping against the rolled-up windows. "Here we are," Sadek announced gaily. "But please do not get out of the car until someone comes. These dogs are very dangerous."

A tall leathery old woman, who wore a long black dress covering her ankles and a black veil across the lower part of her face, approached us from one of the houses. Her clothes were in rags. But in spite of her age she was as straight as a young cadet and moved with the grace of a dancing teacher. She bent forward, picked up a rock, threw it hard and hit one of the dogs, then spoke to them sharply in Arabic. They slunk back and stood there waiting, looking at us from fiery eyes. When Sadek and Jacques jumped out of the car and greeted her she smiled, obviously glad to see them. Sylvia and I climbed out of the car slowly, our eyes on the dogs that had started growling and barking again.

Two young men appeared from one of the houses, and Sadek introduced them. Hussain Dandache, a shy nineteen-year-old, was to be our guide. The other, Essa Dandache, who was slightly younger, was going to guide for Sadek and Jacques. An older man came up over the top of the ravine on the far side of the village. He was dressed in a huge pair of black baggy pants, an Arab headdress of white cloth with a tassled cord wound round the top of his head to keep it in place, and a dark-gray shirt. An ancient long-barreled rifle was slung across his back, and a curved knife hung in its sheath from his belt. He and Sadek embraced, to a large wave of relief on Sylvia's and my part.

Sadek turned and said, "This is my very good friend. We met the first time I came here, two years ago. It was very funny. I was fishing and Jacques was watching me from the bank. Suddenly I glanced up and there was my friend glancing down at me through the sights of his rifle. He said, "I am going to kill you.""

"Never have I been so scared," interrupted the quiet Jacques. "There was no place to run, and he was too close to us."

Sadek let out a peal of laughter. "I said, 'Don't shoot. Come down and talk to me. I have a beautiful apple. I will give it to you.'"

Looking at the sharp-faced outlaw and then at Sadek, I

could imagine the outlaw killing them all right. "And we have been good friends ever since," he concluded.

The outlaw watched us set up our rods. Jacques and Sadek were going to use short heavy spinning rods of glass, while mine was a light fly rod of Tonkin, the first Tonkin, I am sure, ever to find its way into the Beqaa Valley. The outlaw stretched out his hand and I gave him the rod. He waved it gently back and forth, shaking his head.

Sadek said, "He has never seen anything like it. Here they just cut a long bamboo pole and tie a line and leader to the end. But they are good fishermen. Hussain and Essa even fish dry flies, bouncing them on the water from the bank."

The outlaw returned my rod, said goodbye to Sadek and Jacques, and departed over the edge of the gorge. Sadek said, rather proudly, like a father boasting of the talents of a child, "He has killed several men, and when he was younger he stole two of the Jaafirah girls." Then, noting Sylvia's look of horror, he quickly added, "I have explained that you will not take any pictures of him or the other men, so you do not have to worry. He said he hoped you will catch many fish and come back again."

"Come on," Jacques said. "Let's get going. Bob, Hussain will take you and Sylvia through the village and down a path to the river. Sadek and I will go down here and fish up to the source. We all meet for lunch under an olive tree on the other side of the bridge. Good luck!"

They disappeared over the edge of the canyon. Sylvia and I were alone in the land of bandits, unable to communicate with anyone, including our guide. And we were just eighty-five miles from Beirut, one of the world's most cosmopolitan cities.

Since Sylvia and Sadek had brought along picnic lunches for

all of us, Hussain was well loaded. We passed the last house, where a woman was baking Arab bread by flattening globs of dough, plastering them against the inside of an open stone oven, and stacking them on a flat rock when cooked. We accepted one, and tore it up and ate it as we walked to the edge of the canyon.

Then, for the first time, we saw the river, a bright-blue band far below us, twisting like a snake over the desert floor. It had slender borders of stunted trees and shrubs on either side. In most places the downward trail was so narrow we had to go single-file. Sylvia never looked down but moved dizzily at a tortoise's pace, her eyes glued to the canyon wall. After edging past some women who were coming up from the river bearing huge pottery water jars beautifully balanced on their heads, we finally reached the stream. It was in spate— a wild rushing milky torrent of water at least two feet above normal, swirling around the bases of trees and shrubs at the edges of the flooded banks.

For the first hour I never saw a sign of a trout. Then Hussain took my fly in his fingers and shook his head to show that it was the wrong pattern for his stream. He looked over all my flies and finally selected a very small dry fly, a Royal Coachman on a #16 hook. This did not make any sense in this wild rushing torrent. But I tied it on and followed him down the stream. When we came to a small quiet pocket of water where the river had cut into the bank, he pointed. I cast and the fly danced on the riffling surface. A trout splashed as it took. It was a rainbow, about eight inches long.

Sylvia, watching from the bank, said, "Good for you! Now if the bandits kill us it will have been all worthwhile."

By hunting out the occasional bits of quieter water I managed to catch four more. They were all the same size, really too small to take from the stream. Now my broken arm and ribs began to pain, and I signaled to Hussain that I'd had enough. He picked up the lunches and led the way upstream to a narrow bridge, which we crossed. We walked downstream a few rods and settled down on the ground in the shade of a large olive tree. Dark shadows swept along the canyon wall; there was a clap of thunder and it began to rain. Rain in the desert! For five minutes it poured, and new little rivers ran everywhere through the sand. Then it cleared and again the sun blazed through the trees.

Sylvia gripped my arm in terror and said, "Look! The bridge."

There was a large man in a saffron-colored burnoose, a one-piece garment of hood and robe that hung almost to his ankles. He too wore baggy pants, a pair of inlaid black leather boots, a dark shirt, and a sashlike belt around his waist. A short-barreled rifle was slung on his back and the jeweled handle of a dagger in his belt reflected the sunlight. He started toward us.

Sylvia gave Hussain a desperate look. He only shrugged. "My God, he doesn't know him," she said. "Quick— unpack the lunch. Let's try to be natural. And hide that camera."

I shoved the camera into my tackle bag and unfastened the sack that held the lunches. We started setting things out on the ground. As the stranger stepped in under the olive branches I noticed that, unlike the other people we had seen, he was handsomely attired. Along with the new desert boots his burnoose was clean, and obviously it had not been made in one of the desert homes on the ridge.

He opened a gold cigarette case and held it out to me. I took one and nodded my head by way of thanks. He took one for himself and repocketed the case, ignoring Sylvia and Hussain. Sylvia offered him a chicken sandwich. He refused it twice, according to Arab custom, then accepted it.

Sylvia addressed him in French, but he did not understand. Suddenly he turned, glaring, and looked her over very carefully, as though she were an animal he was thinking of buying. He went up to her and fingered her light coat and ran a hand across a shoulder and down one of her arms. I got up off the ground and moved toward him, though what I could have done, unarmed and with my broken arm in a sling, I can't imagine. Then abruptly the stranger turned his back on Sylvia and squatted down to help himself to the food. He consumed half the picnic we had brought along, eating as though starved. Where had he come from? And how had he gotten into this valley? When he finished he glanced at an expensive wrist watch, bowed to me, and left, again disregarding Sylvia and Hussain. Walking downstream, he gradually worked his way up the canyon wall until he disappeared.

When we finished eating Sylvia said, "Let's go back to the village. I really am afraid."

It took us almost an hour to reach the snarling dogs at the top. In front of the first house we reached was a group of women and children. Hussain motioned for us to go in, so we gathered that this was his home. When we pushed aside the curtain over the doorway we noticed the line of tattered sandals on the stone floor. So we removed our shoes and laid them beside the others.

The old woman who had met us that morning was there, along with another about her age, also dressed in worn black. They might be the wives and mothers of men who killed and kidnapped outside the law, but they were two of the most regal and magnificent women we had ever seen. The toughness and character in their lined and weathered faces showed that they were women used to giving commands and to being obeyed. There were also several young women and small children, who stood against a wall looking at us and whispering to each other.

The old woman motioned us to settle on two comforters on the floor of the stone-walled room. Other villagers peered in at us through the shuttered openings. Hussain brought in a boy of his own age who greeted us in French and introduced himself as Ahmad Mattar, the local schoolteacher. With Sylvia's relatively fluent French, and Ahmad acting as interpreter, a varied question-and-answer conversation was carried on between Sylvia and the bandits' women, while primitive and not very clean refreshments were served to the three of us as we reclined on the floor.

I asked Ahmad if anyone other than Sadek, Jacques, Hussain, and Essa fished the Abu Ali, and he said that several of the Dandache men occasionally did. He said they all fished with bait except Essa and Hussain and added, "Those two used to get their trout by dynamiting the pools, but not any more." He translated my question in Arabic and one of the old women laughed, went to the cupboard, pulled open a drawer, and took out six sticks of dynamite. Displaying them in the dim light of a broken kerosene lamp, she explained through Ahmad that the boys had given her these sticks for safekeeping.

The dogs started to bark again. A moment later Sadek and Jacques entered the room and said that we must be getting along. Sylvia and I rose to make our farewell, and each of the old women went up to her and took her face gently between her hands.

In spite of our impending departure from Lebanon we went out once more to the Beqaa Valley with Sadek, Jacques, and two old friends from home, one of whom was teaching at the American University in Beirut. Before this last trip I told one of the Lebanese cabinet officers about our plans to return to the valley. He said, "Sadek Tabbara never should have taken you there. That is probably the best place to get killed on the face of the globe. I wouldn't go into that valley for a thousand pounds. Most of the men in that place would be glad to shoot you for your watches. You should not go back, but if you insist I'll arrange a military escort." We graciously refused the escort. If the army was going into the Beqaa Valley it was not going with us.

It was on the last day of April 1967, just before the Middle East was plunged into war, when we returned to the Upper Region of the Strong Ones. We were laden with gifts for the women and children. Sylvia had spent most of a day shopping in the Beirut bazars for the right kind of cloth and veils for new dresses for the two old women in black. And there were drawing books and crayons, a supply of Arabic schoolbooks for the children, and, of course, a large supply of candy.

Again we caught a number of trout, but none of any size. As the afternoon light took on the yellowish tint of an ending day and shadows crept down the canyon wall, we climbed back to the village and the angry dogs. Once more we ate with Hussain's family. They tried to press gifts on us, two dozen eggs, a pile of Arab bread, a bag of nuts in their shells. They wanted so much to share what they had and give something in return for what we had brought to them. When darkness fell and we had all climbed into the car a pretty girl came running up through the village. She was carrying two live chickens. When we again refused she seemed so sad that Sylvia jumped out of the car, embraced her, and took the chickens.

A few days later we convened with our fishing friends at Beirut's fashionable St. George's Hotel and Sadek cooked our trout in a small Scandinavian smoker on our table. It seemed very civilized and thousands of miles from the Abu Ali, the desert gorge, and a land where a man's status depended on the number of men he had killed and women he had kidnapped and raped and how much deadly narcotics he had grown and smuggled out to the world's markets.

But the next morning the Beqaa Valley was brought to us vividly when we read in the Beirut *Daily Star* that the police had invaded the valley and killed a famous Damascus outlaw who was wanted for a bank robbery and murder. The description of him convinced us that the man they had killed was the one who had stopped to lunch with us under the olive tree.

Sylvia read the piece aloud and slapped the paper onto the table. "He was a stranger in that valley," she said indignantly. "He never had a chance."

The fact that the man had fled to the valley while wanted for murder did not concern her. I too was sorry that he had not escaped to start life anew with the Dandache or the Jaafirah, and perhaps even to learn to cast a fly on the Abu Ali.

✿✿✿ My Cousin Charlie

My cousin Charlie was brought up by a mother who thought fishermen were crazy and by a father who would rather fish than eat. And this is no exaggeration. If his father had gone two days without eating and had been offered his choice between a piece of rare roast beef with all the fixings and a trout stream, he would not have hesitated. He would have just pulled on his waders.

Charlie, who was twice as smart as a whiz kid, amassed education and degrees and finally married the niece of one of America's principal tycoons, a man to whom no one but the niece had ever said "No" and walked out alive. He too loved to fish and agreed with Charlie's father that it was high time something was done about this erring young man. So Charlie went fishing on his honeymoon, fishing for the first time, because his uncle-in-law-to-be, who owned some of the best salmon water on the North Shore of the Saint Lawrence, informed him that that was what he and Jane were going to do. When Charlie told her his honeymoon plans Jane said, "You mouse," and Charlie answered, "Yes, dear."

The honeymoon started a bit on the frigid side, after a church ceremony in which Jane was sorely tempted to respond "Like hell I will" instead of "I do." Jane had wanted to go to Nassau and display her trousseau, not swat black flies.

But black flies were what she swatted, hundreds of them. Charlie fished so that on his return he could tell her uncle that he had done so, while Jane sulked in a camp that had been screened about forty years before and now had more holes than screens. As Jane's uncle said, "If I put in new screens then the flies couldn't get out. Ha, ha, ha!" His real reason was that he did not want to spend the money (after all, he only had a hundred million dollars) because he never used the camp himself during the black-fly season.

Jane's arms ached from swatting. It did not seem possible that there were this many bugs in the whole world, even assuming, as she did, that they had all gathered in this one spot. If she hadn't been so mad at her husband and uncle she would have gone fishing to try to get away from them. As it was, bzzzz bang, bzzzz bang.

Meanwhile, Charlie fished and fished, and, like his wife, wondered why he had made the mistake of getting married. The only good thing about fishing, he decided, was that at least it was preferable to his wife's company. But in my cousin's defense, even if he does have this one loophole in his character, he is basically a gentleman and a nice guy. So at least he tried.

"Why don't you come fishing, dear?"

"Go jump in the river. If you were a man I would be in Nassau." Wham! Another black fly.

So he would take his rod and sneak down the trail to where his guide and the canoe waited.

If salmon had once frequented this river back in the Pleistocene era they apparently had long since found other places to lay their eggs and raise the children. Day after day of waving that silly stick in the air and flinging a mess of feathers first here, then there. And for what purpose? If you wanted a fish that's what fish markets were for. Charlie began to wonder if perhaps his father and cousin Robert, who enjoyed this sort of thing, were not missing some of their parts. And obviously Alphonse, the guide, who insisted the salmon were here but just not taking at the moment, belonged in a place with a high wall around it.

Charlie lived through thirteen days of this without a break. Finally, on the last day, the day when they would be leaving after lunch, praise-the-Lord, Charlie sucked in his breath and tried for the last time. "Darling, there aren't any fish in the river, but it is beautiful and generally there is a breeze, so there aren't many flies."

She snorted.

"Do come and see it, just for an hour."

Whack! Another one. She looked at him. Basically, Jane, like Charlie, was a nice person. Besides, in another two days she would be sitting in Reno. So . . . "All right. For an hour."

Alphonse, who had developed a pretty low opinion of Charlie and his observations concerning man's finest recreation, said, "I'll take the missus. Gerard here will take you. You will drop downstream to the Mill Pool. I will take the missus up to the Ledge Pool."

Jane sat in the bow facing Alphonse so he could admire her swollen and mottled face and her hair matted down with fly dope. She tried not to snarl at him. After all, it wasn't his fault, But Uncle George— oooh! Just wait till she saw Uncle George. She wondered if Brice Tenney still loved her and would be interested in marrying a brand-new divorcée.

"Have you ever fished?" Alphonse inquired.

She shook her head. Maybe Brice would come out to Reno and they could play the slot machines together.

"Now you watch me," Alphonse said. "It is really very easy."

She took the rod. How was she going to break the news to Charlie, she wondered as she waved the rod in the air. If only he hadn't let Uncle George walk all over him so that they wound up here.

"No, not that way," Alphonse said. "Take it easy. Don't let your fly skip over the water like that."

But Alphonse was wrong. A fly skipping over the water apparently was what the salmon had been waiting for all these days.

The next thing Jane knew she was gripping her rod for all she was worth as line sailed off the reel. Then the salmon jumped. To Jane it looked as big as a barn.

"Let him run," Alphonse counseled. "It is a good one."

This was an understatement. The salmon, which an hour later Alphonse netted, was the largest salmon to be taken in the Province of Quebec that year, forty-seven and a half pounds.

When Alphonse beached the canoe, Charlie was there waiting for her. After all, he thought, he had loved her. And there was no reason why they ever had to come back here. Now he could tell her uncle that he had tried but fishing was not for

him. He helped her out of the canoe, failing to notice the very well-filled canvas bag in the stern. "Isn't the river lovely, darling?"

She smiled at him for the first time since he had arranged to honeymoon here. "I'll say. It's pure heaven."

"Hunh!" he said. This was more than he had expected.

"Do we really have to leave today, darling? Couldn't you wire your boss that you broke your neck or something?"

The only reply that Charlie could think of was another "Hunh!"

That was twenty-nine years ago. Next summer Charlie and Jane will celebrate their thirtieth vacation on their thirtieth anniversary in her Uncle George's camp on the river.

In the early days Charlie suggested that it might be fun, just once, to go to Cape Cod or Bermuda.

"Cape Cod? Bermuda? But darling, there aren't any salmon there," she answered, settling that one for good and all.

He sighed. "All right." After all, he did love her for eleven months out of every year. "But don't you think that this year we might put some new screens up?"

"But then how would the bugs get out? Ha, ha, ha!"

So each summer Charlie packs up a head net, gloves, an assortment of fly dopes and a pile of books and sets off, with thanks to heaven that his vacation only lasts a month and that when it ends he and Jane will go back to New York and be in love again.

~~~ Big Game on a Fly

Six of us, old friends, were at the George River Lodge on the big subarctic river of that name. In addition to our group there were two others in the camp, Boogey Spangler (where he acquired the first name we never learned) and Fritz. Fritz's last name I do not recall. Boogey was a tugboat captain from Albany, New York, and Fritz owned a lumberyard in the same city.

We all liked Boogey and Fritz. Boogey was quick-witted and talked all the time. Fritz never said anything. But every time Boogey finished a story he would wind it up by saying, "Isn't that right, Fritz?" and Fritz would nod confirmation. These two had fished the George many times and knew the salmon lies, which they were quick to insist that we share. So, in addition to the excellent stories, we had other reasons for liking them.

~~~~ 100 ~~~~~~~~~~~~~~~~~~~~~~~~~~~~~~~~~~~~~~

All of us were salmon fishing except for Dave Coolidge of Burlington, Vermont, a sixty-two-year-old banker who had fished and hunted over much of the globe. Dave was after a caribou.

I have never seen anyone with luck to compare with Dave's. All the rest of us fished and caught salmon and saw caribou, lots of them. Dave hunted hard, close to fifteen miles a day of hiking up hill and down over muskeg, stuff that allows you to sink into it and then grabs your boots like a vise, without seeing even a calf.

Finally, the day before we were due to head for home, Bill Mott, one of the lodge's co-owners, took pity on Dave. He said, "That guy will never see a caribou where he's standing. I'm going to fly him downstream where he can't miss."

Dave was on the shore about three hundred yards from camp and he was fishing, his rifle beside him just in case. Bill Mott sent one of the guides to get him and flew him far down the river in his Cessna to where he said the caribou were so thick that if you wanted to you could spear one.

I was too lazy that morning to go way upstream or way downstream to the best salmon water. Instead I settled for the spot near camp that Dave had vacated, one that we had learned about from Boogey and Fritz. After an hour or two Boogey and Fritz beached their boat and fished a rod or two below me. As usual Boogey was talking, an uninterrupted flood of words. Occasionally he would pause just long enough to ask, "Isn't that right, Fritz?" As always Fritz would nod assent, then Boogey would start in again.

I landed a salmon, took the fly out of its jaw, and released it. Suddenly I realized that something was wrong. Boogey wasn't talking. I turned my head. There, about seventy feet behind him, was the most magnificent bull caribou I have ever seen.

He had a rack that the American Museum of Natural History would gladly have given the shirt off its director's back, if not the director himself, to own.

Then, to my utter amazement, Boogey started casting, not toward the river but toward the caribou. He made a half-dozen false casts, putting out more and more line, and then a perfect cast. The fly landed right in among the horns and whipped around one of them. Boogey was fast to a caribou.

"Why do you suppose I ever did that?" he yelled.

"Are you planning to tail him or net him?" I inquired.

The caribou bounced into the air like a rubber ball and headed for the hills at top speed. And an animal that can out-run a big arctic wolf without even trying can move across the landscape in a hurry. Fishing writers are wont to describe reels as howling, whining, or screaming. Boogey's reel made a police siren sound like a chipping sparrow.

His rod was pointed in the direction of the fast-vanishing bull. He had thirty yards of tapered casting line and two hundred yards of backing. It was all gone in seconds.

I had figured that when the line came down to the drum on the reel the caribou would snap the leader, but it didn't work that way because Boogey, figuring no salmon would take it all out, had not bothered to knot it.

Boogey turned to Fritz. "The next time someone tells about a salmon taking out line tell him to try a caribou. Isn't that right, Fritz?"

Fritz solemnly nodded confirmation.

At six that evening Bill Mott and Dave Coolidge came back. No, they had not seen a caribou. When Dave heard Boogey's story of his attempt to land one, Dave, a man of typi-cal Vermont restraint, said, "I'll be darned."

ᔍᔍᔍ Roughing It

I was lunching at the Theodore Gordon Flyfishers club with a friend who is one of the world's top big-game hunters, also a fine fisherman. I was telling him about a trip that I planned to take to Argentina, and we fell to discussing the company of ladies in the field. He said, "Women should be against the law on fishing trips. On a hunting trip it's not so bad— you can always shoot them. But if you're fishing and want to rough it you don't want women along."

"Hear, hear!" I agreed. "When I get off the plane and say goodbye to the stewardess, that will be the end of skirts till I fly north again. This is a man's trip— period."

Thirty-six hours later the ordeal had started. I was in a small Buenos Aires night club sipping a glass of champagne while I tried, most unsuccessfully, to listen to George Smith, Pan Am's local manager, comment on my fishing itinerary. A South American had told me to be sure to look George up, that what he didn't know about trout fishing on both sides of the Andes could be printed on top of a thumbtack.

But there was a floor show going on.

George said, "Okay, since you're not listening we'll change the subject. I'll bet you can't equal this show in New York."

"Why New York?" I asked. "You can't equal it anywhere."

The show was composed of some very hot babes, who would have been all set for the showers if they had taken off their shoes.

Finally it came to an end and my pulse started heading back toward normal. George said, "This itinerary is fine except for one thing: you've skipped Chile. You're going to San Martín de los Andes in Argentina. Pucón, in southern Chile, is only a couple of hundred miles from there. And, brother, you haven't lived until you've shot the rapids with a Chilean boatman. This is where they separate the men from the boys, not to mention from the women. I'd better warn you, getting over there is not so easy; it's one tough bus ride. But go anyway and stay at the Antumalal, one of the best hotels in the world, and fish the Liucura River. One day on the Liucura will do the trick. It'll be a trip you'll never forget."

So two weeks later I boarded a rickety old bus in San Martín de los Andes and took off on a nine-hour trip for Pucón over a dirt road that corkscrews in and out and around the mountains and is just wide enough for a motorcycle. There were a number of places where you could have stepped off the bus without touching ground for two hundred feet. Every time we passed one there were a lot of buzzards flying around hopefully, their beaks hanging open.

A plump, aristocratic lady in her seventies, sitting in front of me, turned and said, in excellent English, "Some of the roads in my country, Italy, are bad, but nothing like this."

I asked the lady, who looked as out of place on that bus as a washed face and a haircut on a hippie, where she was going.

She informed me that she was going to meet her husband at some resort about twenty miles from Pucón. I learned that her husband was an Italian diplomat and that she had been traveling all over the world with him for the past forty years. "You'll love Pucón," she said. "It's quite a watering place for Americans."

"How did you know I was an American?" I asked.

She smiled. "I saw them putting your luggage on. No one but an American or Englishman carries that many rods. What do you do, throw a rod away each time you catch something?"

We came to the border customs and immigration station. The Italian lady said, "You don't speak Spanish, do you?"

"Sure I do. *Sí, gracias, uno, dos, tres, martini seco.* With that I get three drinks before dinner."

She said, "That's excellent. You just keep quiet and let me handle everything."

And handle it she did. I had enough luggage to stay in Pucón for twenty years, including lots of things customs men are wild about, four cameras and two dozen color films made in the U. S., for example. My stuff and hers stayed on the bus. Everyone else's had to be lugged inside and opened. I've never seen such a going-over. Apparently a rumor had gotten around that somebody's crown jewels were about to go across the border.

The Italian lady had a diplomatic passport. On top of that she had a way about her. If she had been around at the right time she could have talked Nixon into coming out for

McGovern. She demanded to see the head man, and when he bounced out of his office she walked back into it with him at her heels. When she emerged he came out too, climbed on the bus— I was the only person on it— bowed, saluted, and shook hands. I felt like a visiting king.

The lady climbed aboard and sat down beside me. "Come, let us have our lunch. I have a bottle of very good wine."

"Fine," I said. "But what in the name of heaven did you tell that customs man?"

She laughed. "It was nothing. I just told him that I had inside information that you are a famous banker on a secret mission. You are down here to decide whether or not your country should give Chile fifty million dollars to fix their roads. You know, about two months ago the United States gave Argentina fifty million for their roads and Chile has been jealous ever since. And just in case you didn't know it, you are the man who made all the arrangements. Oh, I had better get off again and arrange for them not to bother you on your way back. When are you returning?"

I told her in two days.

We drank her wine and chatted about places we both knew. She had been everywhere. At the end of a few miles we drove through a big ranch and stopped to take on a female passenger. She was blond, young, tall, and beautiful. She took a seat behind some Indians and opened a magazine.

The Italian lady said, "Go. Go and sit next to her. She is for you."

"For me?" I said. "That girl isn't as old as my son."

"It's all right. The young girls, they like older men. The older men have so much experience. It's men like you who know how to make love. Or if you don't, you should."

I smiled at her. "You have quite an imagination."

"Go," she said. "Your wife will know nothing about it."

I said, "No thanks. When I write, I'll have to confess all about falling in love with an Italian lady on a bus. That's enough trouble for one trip."

She said, "You are hopeless. Also, you are crazy. That girl is very nice."

When the bus arrived in Pucón it didn't seem possible that we had been on the road nine hours.

As I said goodbye, remembering my European manners, which are famous from one end of Hell's Kitchen to the other, I kissed the Italian lady's hand.

She said, "You've been reading travel folders." But being Italian, she liked it just the same.

George Smith had been right: the Antumalal was one of the best hotels in the world. Comfort and luxury were everywhere. There were huge windows overlooking wide lawns, gardens it would take hours to walk through, enough gardeners to guarantee every blossom personal daily attention, and at the foot of the hill, the great, mountain-rimmed Lago Villarrica with long, black beaches of volcanic ash. In the hall hung pictures of distinguished visitors, Adlai Stevenson and Barry Goldwater among them.

After dinner the manager informed me that the trip down the Liucura was set for six the next morning, with breakfast at five-thirty. He said that since he knew I wouldn't mind sharing the trip with an American couple, he had already arranged it.

Well, as it happened, I did mind, very much. In fact, my idea of hell is a beautiful trout stream that you have to share eternally with a bunch of women. But still being flattened out by my surroundings, and mellowed a mite by three martinis and an excellent dinner with a bottle of wine, I said meekly, "No, that's fine."

The next morning I was up at five. There were nine men and one woman in the dining room. Since everyone was speaking Spanish except the woman and her escort, I did some fast detective work and decided this must be the American couple.

Dave Black was a big man, quiet and very deliberate, and he smoked a pipe continuously. He looked like the next headmaster of Groton and obviously was a man a five-year-old girl would be happy to entrust with her last lollipop.

His wife, Lucy, was pretty enough to stuff, very amusing and about half the size of a hummingbird.

Lucy said, "Dave's done a little trout fishing, but I never have. But I've caught dozens of flounders. I suppose it's pretty much the same, isn't it?"

"Exactly," I assured her, wondering just how you would go about taking a flounder on a dry fly. "You won't have any trouble at all. And if I can be of help . . ."

Dave had arranged the lunches, mine included, and seemed to know all about everything. He pulled a map out and showed me where we were and where we would go to launch the boats on the Liucura, about forty miles from town. He explained that we would get down to the lake by the end of the day and then would be driven back to the hotel.

"That is," Lucy said brightly, "if we get through the rapids alive."

A number of trucks were in front of the hotel, already loaded with the sturdy rowboats. Lucy and Dave rode in the front seat of ours, and I sat in back on a pile of cushions with the three boats and boatmen.

An hour later we unloaded and the boatmen carried their heavy craft down a steep bank and slid them into the water. Since Dave and Lucy were going to troll they went on ahead.

My boatman rowed upstream, and I started casting in close to shore. Trees overhung the river on both sides, and in under them trout were feeding all over the place. There were a great many rainbows, but they were all small, seven to nine inches. I stopped fishing to show I wanted to go elsewhere.

A couple of miles farther down, we drifted around a bend and there was Lucy, trolling away in a bright red jacket. She looked neat and very pretty against the dark green water and heavy foliage. As we passed by she asked if I had had any luck and I shook my head. I assumed she had not caught anything either, but I asked her anyway.

Her boatman reached down and held up a pair of rainbows of two to two and a half pounds. "It's my lack of experience," she explained. "You need at least twenty years of no experience to catch these fish. I'm sorry, but I don't think you stand a chance."

"Err . . . uh, what fly are you using?" I asked.

She smiled prettily. "Gracious, how would I know? Is there more than one kind?"

About half a mile farther down we came to a long riffle. As we hit the shallows my boatman whirled the boat upstream, leaned on the oars, came to a dead stop and shouted, *"Aquí,"* meaning, "I have a reputation to protect too. Catch something before I'm ruined."

All right, if that's the way he felt about it. . . . On my first cast I hooked a nice rainbow, about a pound. I took the hook out and dropped it back. My boatman yelled, *"No, no,"* which in English means, "You boob, for you a pound is enormous."

So I caught another one and my boatman grabbed it out of

the net. An hour later when Dave and Lucy came down we had four, all about the same size. It was okay with me; in my book there's nothing wrong with one-pound rainbows, especially if you're not smart enough to catch the big ones.

We took off again, with the other two boats close behind. Suddenly I heard a faint roaring sound. It grew louder and more ominous as we drifted down.

We swung around a bend, and there we were, face to face with the River Styx. I looked at a hundred and fifty yards of raging white water that sloped downhill and bounced along at a merry clip of about ninety miles an hour. Everywhere were big black pointed rocks sending up showers of spray. I glanced at my boatman for reassurance. His expression, lugubrious at best, was that of a man about to make a swan dive off the top of the Empire State Building.

And then we were in it. The word "genius" is insufficient to describe a Chilean boatman. One second we would be running down a wall of water to inevitable destruction; the next, descending on a rock that could have reduced us to toothpicks; and two seconds later I'd be sitting there, happy as a trapped fox, with a wave in my lap while the boat spun around like a top. On we went, scraping, swirling, swooping down, whacking the little rocks but somehow missing the big ones.

We made it and the boatman swung in to shore to bail us out. I went upstream along the bank to get what ghoulish joy I could from watching the Blacks wrestle the elements. First Dave came through, his pipe, which was out, clenched between his teeth, his hands glued to the gunwales. He looked more determined than a bronze bust of Napoleon. Next Lucy came. She was as gay as a lady parachute jumper who, well on her way, has just discovered she left her chute behind.

Their boats pulled up beside mine. Lucy said, "Well! That was more fun than a thumbscrew— I think."

A mile or so farther down we pulled in to shore. Being the outdoor type with countless years of camping experience behind me, I jumped out first onto the hard ground. Only it wasn't hard. I sank to my knees in soft black mud.

The three boatmen all started shouting their heads off. Dave, I now learned, spoke Spanish too. He said, "You got off on the wrong side. You're supposed to walk to high ground on that log— that's why he stopped there."

This advice was deeply appreciated, since I was down to my wallet and about to start singing "Nearer My God to Thee."

After sneaking off to wash my pants, socks, and shoes, I joined Lucy and Dave in the grove, clean but moist.

With a martini in me and a second in hot pursuit, I suddenly realized that we were not about to eat the typical fisherman's lunch put up by the fisherman's inn, consisting of some tired ham and peanut-butter sandwiches with the crusts on, warm beer, and overripe bananas and crumbled cookies for dessert. The boatmen were gathered about a fire barbecuing a lamb. Dave was drawing a cork out of a bottle of red wine, and Lucy was laying out an assortment of stuffed eggs, potato salad, sliced tomatoes and crisp little sandwiches, the sort of fare you get at embassy parties in Washington.

That afternoon about five o'clock we came to a set of rapids that would have scared the shirt off Hercules. They sloped downhill like a ski jump and the water went faster than a Gold Cup boat.

Dave said, "We have to get out and walk around. It's about a mile."

"What do you mean, 'have to'?" Lucy asked. "If I were a

duck I wouldn't even fly over them. But don't you think we ought to shake hands and say goodbye to our boatmen? I mean, just in case . . ."

We walked along the bank a few hundred yards, then sat under a tree by the water's edge to watch our three nice Chileans kill themselves.

The boats came down about fifty yards apart. It was like trying to watch three high-wire acts simultaneously, only worse. Half the time the boats were completely hidden by the enormous rocks and waves.

At long last they made it. Dave said, "Sometimes, when the water level is just right, they'll take you down through."

"How simply wonderful," said Lucy. "I mean that the water isn't right today."

Back at the Antumalal, over cocktails, I suggested to Lucy and Dave that they change their plans and take a bus with me to Argentina. "I hope you don't mind roughing it a bit," I said. "The bus . . . well . . . I can guarantee it will be awful, nine hours over terrible roads. But the fishing should be excellent."

Dave shook his head. "Wish we could, but I'm afraid it's out this time."

Lucy looked around, then leaned forward and whispered, "This is in confidence. Dave is down here to see about loaning Chile money for a road-building program."

"Oh!" I said, very happy that I would not be going through customs in their company.

The next morning at seven I was at the bus depot. It was going to be a broiling hot day and the trip, of course, would be hell. But after all, I'd come to fish, and I am used to sweating it out. "Ah well," I thought, "fishing is really a man's world."

I was supervising the loading of my luggage when I glanced up and saw a female approaching. She was dressed in a bright tight skirt and a snug silk blouse that left absolutely nothing to the imagination. Her dark eyes were big enough to skate on. My heart started racing like the spring on a busted clock.

She said, "Are you the Mr. Weiner?"

I nodded. Who was I to argue? Right then I would have settled for any name in the phone book.

"I do not spoke the Englaish mooch. An old Italian lady— vedy nice— she tell me . . . how you say it? To please to meet you."

I said, "How nice . . . I mean . . . let's sind feats together."

She found one and I collapsed beside her. Nine hours! What a pity it wouldn't last nine days.

A porter got in with a huge picnic basket in one hand and a pail with a towel over the top in the other. She nodded toward the basket. "It is the loonch. The odder, it is the present from your fren'."

I lifted the cloth. There in a hundred ice cubes nestled a bottle of French champagne.

"What you do in Chile?" she asked.

I glanced at the champagne, then looked at her. "I'm roughing it," I said. "I came here after fish."

"For you . . . it is too bad, eh?"

"Yes," I agreed, "it's a hard life."

The driver closed the door and I headed back for the trout of Argentina.

ᛋᛋᛋ Rolling Stone

The second time I was asked to fish the Rolling Stone Club, Bill Yost, an Assistant Secretary of State and my host, suggested that Sylvia and Jono might like to come along.

Rolling Stone, a half-hour's drive from Pittsburgh, was once the country estate of the owner of about a third of Pennsylvania, and so Rolling Stone is no woodcutter's hut. It was built to entertain all of Pittsburgh's rich at any given moment, and things were done on a rather lavish scale — upland shooting, golf, riding trails, a polo field, a swimming pool where you needed field glasses to see who was at the other end, a dining room that would seat the U. S. Senate with spouses, and, of course, a hatchery and a trout stream.

The trout stream, too small to be called a river, too large to be called a brook, was perfect wading water, where, if you had the skill, you were always sure of taking trout because you knew the trout were always there. Indeed, if you were assigned beat 12 and at lunchtime had taken one three-and-a-half-pounder, two of two pounds, and four one-pounders, by the time you had finished your martinis and a snack and returned to the water all of the above trout— exactly the same size— would have been replaced from the hatchery and would be swimming around in various pools on beat 12 waiting for whoever drew the water.

In addition to Sylvia and Jono there was a delightful, very bright Southern gentleman named Peter Pease, Vice President of the World Bank. Of course, Peter Pease was not his real name. Anyway, he was a very knowledgeable man, a fine raconteur, and he could outdrink anyone I have ever known except our host.

All this was back in the days when ships passed through the Suez Canal and the Aswan Dam was yet to be built, but at a time when Nasser had the Aswan dream and was working hard on Peter's World Bank for financing.

When we gathered at the hatchery to be assigned our morning beats, Bill Yost suggested that Sylvia might like the services of a guide. The rest of us, all experienced fly fishermen, could get along on our own. Trout fishing always puts me in an expansive mood, so I promptly nodded, not having sense enough to ask what the guide would cost.

I learned when we quit for the morning and gathered along the roadside to be picked up by Bill Yost and his car. Eighteen bucks. Eighteen bucks for two and a half hours of taking an occasional fly out of a tree. I said, "This afternoon, sweetie, you don't need a guide. If you get hung up in a tree, break your fly off and leave it there. Flies are fifty cents apiece, and you certainly are not going to get hung up out of reach thirty-six times." She agreed.

The morning had been a good one. Between the five of us we had accounted for twenty trout, including the seven Jono caught and returned to the river. At the club we sat on the five-acre terrace. Sylvia had a Dubonnet, Jono a glass of beer, the rest of us martinis, and we discussed the fishing and the multi-billion-dollar Aswan Dam that the World Bank was just about to underwrite, mostly, of course, with U. S. funds. The first martini tasted so good that I had a second, and Bill Yost and Peter Pease each managed to put four away before we got down to the chicken sandwiches and coffee. As Bill said, we ought not to fool around eating, we ought to get back to the trout.

After lunch, instead of resorting to the couch, which the older men, this one included, would have favored for a couple of hours of siesta, we returned to the hatchery to learn which were our beats for the afternoon. The reason we eschewed the midday slumber was that Bill Yost had failed to make room reservations ahead, so every bed in the club was taken and we were staying at an inn thirty-five miles away.

At six o'clock Bill picked us up in the reverse order of that in which we had been dropped. I was first and had five trout to show, of which I was rather proud, having only fished an hour and a half before succumbing to a mossy bank with a hump at the top like a pillow. Bill Yost and Peter Pease had both gotten skunked. I did not comment on the leaves and twigs adhering to their backs. Jono had gotten eleven, including a brown of four and a half pounds that he had weighed in his net before releasing.

The last to get in the car was Sylvia, on a beat at least two miles up the road from the rest of us. She was sitting on a log with her tear-streaked face between her hands. She had a pound-and-a-half trout under a pile of stones, which she pointed out to Jono. "Will you get it? I don't ever want to touch another one of those things again."

Up to that time Sylvia had not done much fly fishing, and what she had done had always been from a canoe in Canada with a guide. The guide had always killed the fish. So this afternoon Sylvia had started fishing and in the first pool had hooked her brown. Finally she netted it, and from there she should tell the story, and if it doesn't make you cry it's her fault, not mine.

"I tried to take it out of the net with a piece of Kleenex, but every time I touched it it wriggled," she said. "Then it would look up at me and go 'Uhhhhhh!' So finally I took it ashore and dropped it out of the net on the bank. Poor thing! It kept bouncing around, looking up at me and going 'Uhhhh!' I found a stick, but every time I went to grab it it would flop around and look up at me and go 'Uhhhhh!' again."

She began to sniffle. "So I did the only thing I could think of, I threw stones at it. But it kept right on looking at me and making those little moaning sounds. I began to cry so hard I couldn't see to hit it. Then I knelt down in front of it and shouted, 'Die, damn you, die,' It took forever." Her eyes filled up with tears and she blew her nose hard. "I've never had such an awful afternoon. I'm never going to fish again."

"I suggest we get back to the inn and dine there," said Peter Pease. "They put more gin in their martinis than the Rolling Stone. And I think the food is all right."

"You're right," agreed Bill Yost. "Their drinks are nearly twice as strong. And we'll eat Bob's trout for dinner, and that one of Sylvia's that talked so much."

It is amazing how fast fishermen can get cleaned up with the thought of that first martini ahead of them. Sylvia had barely enough time to mop the tears off her face and hadn't

touched her hair or started on that endless time-consuming female job of applying makeup by the time Jono had downed
half a glass of beer, and I was into my second martini and Bill
and Peter were polishing off round three. By the time I was
into my fourth and Bill and Peter had reached the decision
that one more wouldn't hurt them and were involved in round
six, Sylvia appeared, neat as a pin, took one look at me and
said, "You've had enough. By the time you finish that one
you'll talk all night in your sleep and Jono and I will have to
drive home tomorrow, three hundred and twenty miles."

I said, "Yes, dear," and sipped quickly.

"Been a nice day," Peter announced, his words slightly
blurred. "Don't know what's wrong with your fishing and
mine, Bill. This kid catching all those fish and we don't catch
anything." He shook his head and said, "Awful." He took a
long gulp of his seventh drink, finished it, and his head
slumped forward on his chest. He was out cold.

Bill Yost, who can outdrink a convention of bartenders, said,
"He's all right. Just let him sit there and rest. After a while
he'll come around. Maybe the rest of us better eat. Or Bob,
would you like another drink?"

"No," said Sylvia, "he wouldn't."

Jono reached out and caught the Vice President of the
World Bank by his shirt front just in time to keep him from
sliding under the table. He propped him up and pushed his
chair in till the table pressed against his chest.

"Maybe you ought to take his belt off and fasten him to the
back of his chair," suggested our host. "Then if no one is
watching him he won't slide down and bang his head on the
floor. Here, I'll do it." And, in spite of six martinis, he did,
looping the belt around Peter and a rung in the back of the
chair.

The World Bank's Vice President slumbered on, his chin against his chest. I wondered how we would ever get him to bed.

We were halfway through a good steak dinner when the pretty inn manageress came to our table and announced, "There is a long distance call from Washington for Mr. Pease. Something about the Suez Canal. Someone called Natzer, or something like that, has taken it. The call is from a Gordon Knott and he says he has to talk with Mr. Pease right away." She looked down at the slumbering Peter and grinned.

Bill said, "Knott is the bank's P. R. man. Tell him to talk to Al Brooks, the bank's President. Tell him Mr. Pease is asleep and left a message that he does not want to be disturbed."

Thirty seconds later the lady manageress was back. "Mr. Knott says the President of the bank can't be located. And neither can the Executive Vice President. He says to put some ice water on Mr. Pease's head. He says no matter how drunk he is he has to talk to him. All the papers and T. V. stations want an immediate statement."

"Bob, you and Jono wake him up. I need a breath of fresh air," Bill announced, pushed back his chair and was gone.

I gave the Executive Vice President a hearty shake.

"Careful," Sylvia said. "You may shake his head off."

"Mr. Pease," Jono shouted, as if announcing the train for Atlanta. "Nasser has nationalized the Suez Canal."

All heads in the dining room turned, including Peter Pease's. "What?" he bellowed. He tried to jump up, but being fastened to his chair he didn't get very far. "What?"

Jono told him again. "A Gordon Knott is on the phone. Can I help you?"

"Yes. Get me out of this goddam straightjacket. This is vital. This is the end of the Aswan Dam so far as the bank and the

U. S. are concerned." He banged his fist on the table. "That son of a bitch. We ought to send in the marines."

Jono and I were struggling with the belt, which had been tightly fastened. And Peter's gyrations were no help. I tried to cut it with a steak knife and got nowhere. Finally Jono made it and Peter was on his feet. "Where's that phone?"

The Vice President, out to the world three minutes earlier, now dictated at least a thousand words into a tape recorder in his P. R. man's office. He even dictated the punctuation. The next day the statement was on the front page of every paper from Portland, Maine, to Portland, Oregon. It was the clearest press release I have ever read. Just like that the decision was reached to withdraw all further support for the Aswan Dam.

The inn dining room was full of people who gazed with wonder at the man dictating into the wall phone in his underpants, his trousers piled around his ankles.

When he finally hung up he said, "That should hold 'em." He reached down and pulled up his pants.

Bill Yost said, "Good job. Let's have one more to celebrate."

"Good idea," I added.

Sylvia emitted a low moan.

Jono put his arm around her. "This time Sylvia and I will join you." And they did.

The Russians eventually built the Aswan Dam, and it has leaked like a spigot ever since. And Sylvia finally learned to kill her own trout, but that's another story.

ᴔᴔᴔLady Fly Fisher

A week after her experience at Rolling Stone, Sylvia forsook her resolution never to fish again and went up to Quebec with me for two weeks at our club. But a guide handled and killed all her trout. So she wasn't faced with the horrendous problem of gripping one of the wriggling slimy things and banging it on the head until she fished Helen Nefferts's pond in our home town of Washington, Connecticut.

That day she learned how to handle and dispatch her own fish.

The evening before, Helen Nefferts, a superb fly fisher in her seventies, and about as lovable a lady as ever lived, called and asked Sylvia to lunch. She said, "And bring your rod and wear fishing clothes. A few of us are going to fish."

Sylvia had no trouble spotting the handwriting on the wall. She told me, "This is a test. I know because before I can become a candidate for membership in the Lady Anglers I have to have fished in the company of at least three members. Oh dear! Thank goodness they hardly ever catch trout in that pond. So they won't expect too much of me. And besides, how would I ever kill one if I did hook it? Tomorrow morning you have to give me a casting lesson on the lawn."

The morrow dawned, bright and windy, a strong steady wind out of the northeast. "Better use your four-ounce rod," I said. "And I'm going to give you a heavy line with a torpedo head so you can lay it out in this wind. I'll put in your two-and-a-half-ounce Orvis rod and a light line just in case the wind dies. But I'm afraid it won't."

"And put a short leader on the line for both reels, not an inch over seven feet," she said.

This I did, at least for the four-ounce rod, and she practiced on the lawn and performed handsomely. I said, "You won't have any trouble at all, just as long as you manage not to catch a fish. When you get there, tie on a Silver Doctor. No brown trout in his right mind would touch it, at least not in that pond."

A few minutes later she took off with all her tackle. Alas, I had forgotten to cut back the leader on the light floating line, a line I used on a two-ounce rod. The leader was twenty feet long and tapered to 7X. This, by error, was the line, leader, and reel Sylvia selected for the heavy rod, a #4 line that was two sizes too light for it, even if there had not been a breath of air instead of a twenty-mile-an-hour blow.

At the lunch were a number of ladies dressed to the teeth who were not going to fish, and four, Sylvia included, clad in khaki pants, who were. One was Dorothy Geoffrey, a formidable lady of eighty-three, President of the Lady Anglers, whom at that time Sylvia had never met; then there was

Helen, who had proposed Sylvia for membership; and the last of the fishing quartet was Barbara Buttrick, a lady in her upper seventies who had won the club's casting championship the last two years in a row, meaning that she handled a fly rod about as well as the late Joe Brooks.

After lunch the ladies in all their fluff went home, and the four in pants marched down the hill to the pond. And so, nervous as a little girl at her first party, Sylvia first selected the wrong reel, and then instead of tying on a Silver Doctor she chose a Light Cahill nymph on a #14 hook.

Helen Nefferts walked down the shore a few yards and started casting into the teeth of the gale. Dorothy Geoffrey, the club President, announced that she was not going to fish, just watch. She was equipped with a notebook and pencil.

"Come on," said Barbara, "you fish from the boat. I'll paddle you around."

Sylvia, her heartbeat too fast to count, climbed into Helen's tiny metal boat and Barbara, with the skill of an Indian guide, paddled out to the center of the pond into the midst of the hurricane.

Sylvia pulled the leader through the guides, yard after yard after yard of it, and tried to cast. The fly landed about two feet from the boat in a snarl of leader and three feet of line, and the fly headed for the pond's bottom. Sylvia, wondering what was wrong— things had gone so well earlier on the lawn— retrieved the mess and was fast to a two-pound brown.

Happily Sylvia knows what to do with a hooked fish, and she played this one to the complete satisfaction of the lady with notebook and pencil standing on the dock. Three minutes later Sylvia scooped it up in her net. She glanced at the kicking fish, then at the president on the dock, then at Barbara Buttrick.

"May I kill it for you?" Barbara asked. "That was very nicely done."

"Biggest trout anyone has caught here this year," Helen Nefferts shouted from the bank. "Good work."

Sylvia glanced again at that thrashing trout, then again at Barbara. "No thanks," she said, "I'll take care of it." She started to shut her eyes, then realized she mustn't. So, like a Japanese, deciding the time is now to stick the knife in and commit hara-kiri, she reached into the net and grabbed the wriggling trout with two hands around its middle and banged its head against the gunwale. She conquered a strong desire to upchuck, removed the fly, and for the first time noticed what she had tied on. My goodness, it was a nymph, not a Silver Doctor at all.

She tossed the trout into the stern of the boat, dipped her hands in the water, washed off the slime and dried them on the seat of her pants. "I had a feeling a Cahill nymph would do the trick," she said.

"You're a smart girl," Barbara commented. "I never would have thought of it myself this late in the season."

Two more casts of that lengthy leader that traveled nowhere in the wind and Sylvia was fast to another. As my friend Sparse Grey Hackle has written, ladies may often outfish men, but return a trout to the water, never. So Sylvia now took the bit in her teeth and did what she had so often seen the Canadian guides and her husband do: she broke the trout's neck with her thumbnail. Suddenly she was a pro. And she knew it.

"Now," she said, "it's your turn to fish and I'm going to paddle."

Somehow the ladies changed places without turning the tiny craft upside down. Barbara took Sylvia's rod and Sylvia took Barbara's paddle— to paddle a boat for the first time and from the bow. Barbara tried a cast, then said, "My dear, I think you have the wrong line for this rod. Don't you have another reel?"

So that was the reason her casts hadn't traveled more than an arm's length, and that was the reason for that horrible long leader. "Of course," she said. "How silly of me. Let's go in and change." She dug her paddle into the water and the boat spun round like a top.

Barbara said, "Here, let me show you how to paddle— not easy in this wind."

The reel changed, the ladies again took to the pond and Sylvia's casting did her credit. They took turns with the rod, but neither one of them caught another trout, nor did Helen Nefferts from the shore. The long 7X leader all curled on the surface had allowed the nymph time to sink all the way to the bottom where the trout were feeding before Sylvia could draw it through the guides. And as she had finally raised her fly off the bottom the fish had taken.

A week later Sylvia learned that she had become a member of the Lady Anglers. And since that day she is one of the few ladies I know who can handle and kill trout like a Maine guide.

ᔕᔕᔕTarpon Guide

In Tampico, Mexico, there is a restaurant called Johnny's, run by an American and his mother, where you can get the best crabs you ever ate as well as up-to-the-minute information on the hunting and fishing all the way south to the Panama Canal. I walked in there in January and the first thing I learned was that I had arrived five years too late for the tarpon.

"Wouldn't care to shoot a few ducks?" asked a Texan I had just met. "Still plenty of those around— pintail, widgeon, blue-bill, teal, gadwall . . ."

I shook my head. "Not this trip. I'm after tarpon and maybe a few snook."

"You're wasting your time, friend," he drawled. "Tampico used to have the best tarpon fishing in the world, right here in the Panuco River. Snook and yellowtail too. But it's all gone—

commercial netting and dynamite. Only place you'll find tarpon around here now is on the hotel ashtrays."

He pushed his plate back and tilted his chair. "But the duck hunting, that's something else again. I been out four days and got my limit every day before noon. Fifteen birds a day. Don't suppose you brought a gun along?" he asked. "Reckon I can help you out. I got a sixteen-gauge I use for quail down here."

I was tempted but finally decided against the gun and stuck to the business I had come for, tarpon and snook.

I asked Johnny if he knew where I could get a boatman.

Johnny said, "Yes, I'll have him here in half an hour, before you finish your dinner."

And a half-hour later the door swung open and in walked my guide. He glanced at Johnny, then came over to my table and sat down.

His name was Pedro. He was a small man, very quick in his movements. His whole face constantly lit up as he smiled. He said that he owned a truck, trailer, and outboard, all we needed, and added, "I think tomorrow will be a very good day for the tarpon. Perhaps you will catch a very big one. It will not surprise me at all."

I arranged to go twenty miles upstream to Tarpon Bend, a few years earlier one of the most famous tarpon holes in the world. He would meet me at eight the next morning, and if I could have finished my breakfast before that time . . .

The next morning at quarter of ten Pedro appeared, sat down, and accepted a cup of coffee. A very sad thing had happened, he told me. His truck, which had never let him down before, this morning refused to work. "It is too bad," he said. "It is the battery. Perhaps if you could advance me some money . . ."

I gave him a hundred pesos. He beamed. "In no time I will have the battery." And he was off.

At a quarter of eleven he was back, all smiles. "We are ready. We now have only to go and pick up the boat."

Pedro's truck, a Ford pickup with no mudguards and a single headlight which bounced up and down as the mufflerless engine fired away on three or four of its cylinders, was nice and cool. This coolness mingled with much dust was occasioned by a windshield that was elsewhere except for a few remnants of jagged glass about the frame. I sat on a wooden board next to Pedro and we bounced through town, bang, pause, bang bang, pause, bang.

It only took half an hour to get the trailer attached and the boat tied on. Shortly after noon we staggered out of Tampico and by one o'clock were at Tarpon Bend.

We launched the boat and Pedro ran it slowly upstream while I cast close in to the shores. Black iguanas, two and a half feet long, gazed at us from the gravel banks or scurried to safety beneath the twisted roots of overhanging trees. An Indian woman was doing the family washing while her naked children splashed about nearby.

Pedro said, "It is too hot to fish. I think it is better to have some lunch."

We went ashore and under a huge shade tree ate our sandwiches and drank some Cokes. When I started for the boat Pedro assured me that it was still much too hot to be on the river. He said, "I think the best plan for now is to take a siesta."

It was after three and I had only fished an hour. Still, there wasn't a cloud in the sky nor a breath of a breeze; also, apparently, there wasn't a fish in the river. I lay back on the ground and closed my eyes. An hour or so later we were awakened by

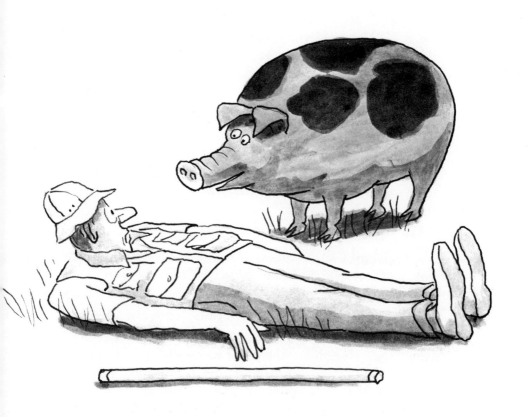

the sound of loud grunting. We were surrounded by feeding hogs. I suggested to Pedro that we go back to fishing. I didn't particularly care for the look of the hogs.

"It is still too hot," said Pedro. "However, if you wish it."

We went fishing. In three hours of trying we caught nothing. "They are not biting today," Pedro announced. "It is most unusual. Only five years ago, a man fishing with me in this boat caught eight tarpon in one day. It is hard to understand. Perhaps it will be better tomorrow."

He looked at me hopefully. I told him that I had a business appointment in Vera Cruz but that I planned to come back to Tampico again some day.

He understood. He shook his head. "I guess it is hopeless," he said. "Six years ago I owned a big boat and three outboards like this. They were busy all the time. Now no one wants to fish here any more."

It was late afternoon but the sun still beat down on our heads, and the river, big, slow-moving, and slate-colored, was without a ripple. Suddenly masses of gray clouds rose above the horizon and raced toward us across the sky, and we could see whitecaps and churning water moving upstream our way. A minute later we were plowing through three-foot waves and the temperature had gone down like a sinker. Thirty seconds before it had been much too hot for comfort and now it was freezing. The spray splashed over the bow, soaking us to our skins, and the eighteen-foot boat danced around on the whitecaps so the propeller was frequently clean out of water.

We made the landing but the boat was so heavy with water it was all we could do to pull it up, turn it over, and get it on the trailer.

"I think maybe it will almost freeze tonight," said Pedro. "I am afraid now the fishing will be no good for several days."

I looked at him, a man in his middle thirties with his business ruined, living already in a glorious past that presumably never would return to Tampico, still hoping for each day to be like the days before the netting and dynamite.

It was getting dark and Pedro discovered that his taillight was not working. He grabbed it and gave it a good shake. It came off in his hands. He gazed at it a moment, shrugged, and tossed it into the back of his truck.

We rattled away from the big river, our one headlight sending forth a faint yellow shaft that moved this way and that like an eye looking the situation over. Finally we reached the main road and turned toward Tampico. The temperature must have been in the low forties. I have never been so cold. Being dressed for tropical weather, wringing wet, and having no windshield didn't help.

The engine seemed to be on the verge of its last bang. The pauses between explosions were longer and it sounded very much as if we were down to two cylinders and occasionally one.

There was a good deal of speeding traffic on the road, and why we weren't run over is hard to fathom. Apparently the Mexicans are all excellent drivers and accustomed to unspeakable crises such as we were. Pedro never got our truck over twenty miles an hour, and as we had no taillight and just that single sad apology for a headlight, and since the wind was blowing clouds of sand across the road, we must have been harder to spot than a potato bug on a Persian rug. Trucks, cars, and buses moving along at sixty to seventy miles an hour would come up behind us, skid almost to a halt, their brakes shrieking, then swerve around us and roar by. Some interesting Spanish words were generally shouted in our direction.

In addition to the possibility of having a truck or bus plow through us as if we were part of a dust cloud, there was another problem. Would this gasping, dying piece of machinery ever make Tampico? And if it didn't, what then? Certainly no one in his right mind would ever stop and give us a ride on that forlorn landscape. I am sure no two people ever looked more like holdup men. We would just pick up forty pounds of camera equipment and tackle and stumble along until we dropped, frozen stiff as boards.

"My truck, it does not seem to be working very well this evening," said Pedro. "I think perhaps something is wrong with it."

I nodded, my teeth chattering too hard for unnecessary comment.

Pedro said, "I think I will stop and look at the headlight. Perhaps I can make it better."

Suddenly my teeth stopped chattering. "Don't," I said. I could see the thing coming off in his hands, and him looking at it with that hurt expression he wore when his equipment let him down.

Far ahead there was a glow of light— Tampico, right then that most beautiful of all cities. Light! Warmth! Tampico!

Bang, pause, bang bang, a longer pause, another bang. But our little truck hung on, determined to die in its own garage. Finally we wheezed and coughed into town. Ah, I thought, in five minutes I'll be at the hotel. I imagined running a hot bath. I could hear the water hissing out of the faucet. Just four minutes to go. My room presumably would be as warm as toast. Now it can't be more than three minutes, I thought. I closed my eyes. A spot of rum in a glass of steaming hot water. I rolled it around on my tongue. Two minutes left at the very most. There was a loud whistle and a policeman stepped off the curb.

Pedro and the policeman exchanged hundreds of words of furious Spanish. Then Pedro got out. When he and the policeman reappeared, Pedro was stuffing his wallet back in his pocket and the policeman seemed in a much better mood. He turned and left us.

"Ah, that thief, that no good rat," said Pedro. "And for what? For nothing. A terrible situation. And that you, my employer, should see such a thing."

"What did he stop you for?" I asked. "No muffler, or your lights?"

"None of those things," said Pedro. "That crook, that son of an alligator. It was a nothing, it was only that I do not have the license plates."

The next morning I packed and called the airline to confirm my seat to Vera Cruz. No luck. I was politely reminded that I was supposed to call twenty-four hours before flight time. Now, if I would care for a seat on the morrow . . .

I went to Johnny's for breakfast, hoping that I would run into the duck hunter from Texas and perhaps get a bit of shooting. But I was the only customer. Johnny wandered over from behind the cashier's counter, pulled out a chair, sidewise to the table, and stretched out his long legs. "How'd it go?" he asked.

I told him. He nodded. "Pedro's right. The netting hasn't done the tarpon fishing much good. It's illegal to kill them in the nets, but that doesn't seem to stop them. They killed so many they opened a plant to make them into chicken feed. Anyway, you're too early, much too early. April and May are the months."

My breakfast came and Johnny told the girl to bring him a cup of coffee, then asked, "How'd you like Pedro?"

"Very much."

"Did he tell you how he lost his boats, his home, every-thing?"

"No," I answered. "I had supposed that it was the netting and dynamiting that ruined him."

The girl put down his coffee and went back to the kitchen. "He lost them in the flood," Johnny said. "And he got a medal doing it. Poor little bastard, he worked his boat about twenty hours a day. Ask him about it. He'll be in after a while. He knows I send all my fishermen to him. So he comes in to see if there's any business and he takes a cup of coffee. That's all, nothing else. He's always just eaten. I don't suppose he's had a real breakfast for five years."

Johnny drank his coffee and set the cup down. "Someday I suppose Pedro will kill someone in that damned truck, or that old boat will go down and drown him and his customer. But until it happens he gets the business.,"

The restaurant door opened and four Texans came in, among them my duck-hunting friend. He came over. "Like to go out with me for a while this morning? You'll get yourself some ducks."

Suddenly, as quick as that, I changed my plans.

I said, "Thanks a lot. But I'm going to give the tarpon one more whirl."

The Texan shook his head. "You sure don't know when you're licked, do you?"

Half an hour later, Pedro came in, wearing the same torn dirty shirt and pants he'd had on the day before. He sat down at my table and the waitress brought him a cup of coffee. He said, "You have to leave today? It is too bad. I thought it was going to be very cold, but no, it is warm. I think today will be a fine day for fishing. Today they will bite for sure."

I told him that I didn't have to leave after all until the next day. So I was set to fish.

He brightened up like a new quarter. "I think by the railroad bridge will be good for tarpon." He added quickly, "We will not need the truck. It is only four miles from here. One mile to the boat in a taxi and three miles to the bridge. And this evening I will take you to the Yacht Club and they will phone for another taxi. And for sure you will get a tarpon. That much I know."

I went back to the hotel, unpacked my gear, and put on my fishing clothes. On the way to the railroad bridge I asked about the flood.

"Ah, the flood. It was terrible, a terrible thing. And your Red Cross, if it had not been for them I do not like to think of what would have happened. We Mexicans, we will always be glad for your Red Cross."

"I understand you got a medal," I said.

He nodded. "Yes, a medal. For what? I had a boat. What was a man with a boat supposed to do, let the people drown or die in the trees?"

Gradually the story of Tampico's flood unfolded.

The whole town, except for a few of the better houses on a rise of land, had been under water. He told me that Johnny's restaurant right in the center of town had had water up to the ceiling.

"And the people. I would find whole families in trees. But after a while when I got to them many of them were dead. Most often the man would be gone. For a day, maybe two or three days, he would stay there with his wife and the old people and the children in the branches, and then he would go to try and get help. But he would never get it. The currents, they were very strong. And then your Red Cross came to Tampico. What a wonderful country to charge us nothing."

I asked, "Was this the boat you used?"

"Yes," he said. "My other boats, the flood took them. And then, after the flood . . ." He shook his head. "It was awful. Mud. Everyplace there was mud. And snakes, you cannot imagine the snakes. They were in every house that was left. There must have been more than a million of them. Never has anyone seen such a supply of snakes in Mexico. Ah, look, there is the bridge. Today for sure there will be tarpon."

We ran upstream in the boat. When we reached the bridge, on the downstream side, there were two long dugouts. In the stern of each was an Indian working a throw net. The Indians held the tops of the nets in their teeth after drawing them in, and arranged them just so, in a way that was a mystery to me, then they took the tops of the nets in their hands, whirled them around their heads, and let go. They spread out in big circles and landed in the water with a soft swish. The Indians let out rope until they sank to the bottom, then, hand over hand, they pulled them in.

There was not a cloud in the sky. Gulls wheeled in the air, complaining in raucous voices. And the two silent Indians whirled the nets around their heads, around and around, then let them sail out in billowing domes of cord. At the end of twenty-some throws one of them pulled up a fish.

"Ah, a tarpon," said Pedro. "It is a good sign."

The Indian took the baby tarpon, about a ten-pounder, out of his net, whacked it on the head with a club, and went on with his fishing.

Pedro looked over my tackle and picked out a brown-and-yellow plug, and I fastened it on and started casting. Now the second Indian brought in a baby tarpon.

"What do they do with them?" I asked. "Do they eat them?"

"Sometimes. But these, I think they will be sold for crab bait."

"Isn't that against the law?" I asked.

Pedro nodded. "But it is not important. The Indians, they have always done it. It is only the big nets that do us the damage, the nets that go all the way across the river and down to the bottom and are pulled by heavy boats. They fish for yellowtail and snook for the markets, but they catch all of the big tarpon in the river too. Four years ago a man in a small boat like this could fill it in a day with the yellowtail and snook. And the big tarpon, by now you would have at least two in the boat— eighty, ninety, maybe one of more than a hundred pounds."

Close by I saw a little tarpon swirl on the surface. I cast but it didn't take. Another one swirled on the other side, close in to the dugouts, and I cast to him.

Pedro dug around in his rusty tackle box and pulled out a battered red-and-white plug. "Try this. I have caught many fine tarpon on this."

I tried it for half an hour without a strike and without seeing a sign of another fish. Meanwhile the Indians had pulled up their anchors and paddled away.

Pedro said, "The tarpon should be biting now, but it is a bad time of year. Perhaps if we were to eat our luncheon . . ."

I suggested that we go ashore on a rocky point just above the bridge. We ate our sandwiches, then Pedro lay back, put his hat over his face, and was sound asleep. I rigged up my fly rod, put on a yellow-and-red streamer, and tried casting from the shore but could not reach the deep water.

I sat on a rock by the edge of the river and lit my pipe. A

long train rumbled over the steel bridge. Two small boys appeared out of nowhere with cheap rods no more than a yard in length and a can of bait. They scrambled over the rocks until they were almost under the bridge, baited their hooks, and cast out into the water swirling around a stone pier. One of their rods bent like a horseshoe and a three-pound snook shot up into the air. The little boy's reel was a sorry affair, and it promptly backlashed. He dropped his rod and hauled the fish in hand over hand. Both boys fell on it for fear it would bounce back into the river.

About a hundred feet in front of me I saw a tarpon swirl, then again. The water bubbled and rippled as a school of little fish tried to get away. I went over and woke Pedro.

When we were out in the current I picked up my fly rod. Pedro said, "This afternoon you will get one, I am almost certain of it. But I would use the plugs. I have never seen anyone catch the tarpon on the fly."

I said, "I'll try a plug later, but let's give the fly a whirl first."

"You are my employer, it is as you wish it, but I have no optimism about the fly. The plug, it is much the most successful way to catch tarpon."

After a while another baby tarpon rolled about thirty feet from the boat. I cast six feet in front of it and started retrieving fast. The water boiled and the fish came down on the fly like a sledge hammer, ripped fifteen or twenty feet from the screaming reel, and careened up into the air. It weighed perhaps nine or ten pounds, but it was incredibly strong and fast. It jumped seven times. Finally it tired and I brought it in. Pedro gaffed it, driving the steel point up through its lower jaw.

"Ah!" Pedro said. "Didn't I tell you? Today I knew they would bite. When I got up and looked at the sky I was sure of it." He picked up a wooden club.

I said, "No, put it back."

"But this is your first tarpon from the great Panuco River."

I nodded. "Right! And it was good fun. But put it back just the same."

Pedro took the hook out, held the tarpon in his hands, and looked at me sadly to make sure I was determined to make such an awful mistake, then slid the fish over the side.

We rose no more, nor did we see another one swirl. At six o'clock we went in to the Yacht Club. I paid Pedro and gave him half a dozen of the red-and-yellow streamers, as he had now decided that this was much the best lure for tarpon at this particular time of year.

He said, "Next year perhaps you'll come back again. I think next year the Panuco River will have a great many tarpon, and many of them very big ones. I think the netting, it will all be stopped. Yes, I am sure of it because I myself am going to write a letter to the government in Mexico City."

I got in the cab and the driver backed up and turned around. I looked at all the privately owned boats, a dozen or so tied up to the dock by the Yacht Club float— the tarpon fleet that now was seldom used and was badly in need of repairs and paint. And close by was Pedro in his own sad apology for a boat. As we started off I waved to him, but he didn't see me. He was bailing with a small can, scooping the water up and tossing it over the side. He was singing.

That night again I dined at Johnny's. When I told him about the tarpon he said, "I'll be damned." He tilted his chair back and grinned at me. "I probably shouldn't tell you this, but I'm going to. That tarpon of yours is the first one Pedro has boated for the last two years. And I've sent more than thirty parties to fish with him."

I took out my wallet and counted out twenty-five dollars. "For the next month, or until it runs out, give Pedro some eggs and toast with his coffee. Tell him it's on me to celebrate our tarpon."

Johnny nodded, folded the bills, and put them in his pocket. "Maybe if he eats eggs and toast on you for a while he'll get used to it and take some from me."

✿✿✿ Rainbows in Japan

About fifteen years ago a good friend of mine, Ben Swathmore, the senior partner of a large Tokyo law firm, succeeded in establishing the first private trout club in Japan. The Japanese are superb fishermen with their long delicate poles, but until Ben came on the scene fly fishing was unknown to them except for the terribly tied flies they produced for the export market, supposedly copies of U. S. and British products. The best one I have ever seen wouldn't fool a goldfish face to face with starvation.

Ben and his wife Mary were fishing a quarter of a mile below me when I waded into the run-off of a beautiful long pool. On one side was a ledge that went straight up for fifteen feet to the edge of a farm, and on the other side was a low tree-lined bank that separated the stream from the road. The pool was a few rods from the center of a small town.

I saw a swirl as a rainbow took an insect from the surface. I caught one of the insects and, after studying it and looking over everything in my fly box, tied on a Blue Dun on a #18 hook. On my fourth cast a trout rose and I missed it. A low moan went up. Until then I had thought I was alone. I looked up and saw twenty men, women, and children lining the bank by the road. They leaned against bicycles or trees, or squatted by the stream side. Over the edge of the other bank, the one that rose straight up from the water, leaned a little old peasant woman. She stuck out almost straight from the bank, nearly parallel with the water. She gripped the handle of an adze. The blade was hooked over a branch that also hung out over the pool. I expected her to land with a large splash in the center of operations at any moment.

I cast again, and again the trout rose. But I was late; I had had one eye glued on the octogenarian suspended above me like a small cloud. Again a great moan rent the silence.

A policeman on a motor scooter chugged up to find out what was going on. He strode officiously into the crowd's midst, firing questions. They shushed him up and pointed at me. He immediately stopped his engine, spoke in a whisper, and squatted on the bank with the rest of them. In Japan everyone respects a fisherman.

A third time the rainbow rose to my fly. This time I hooked it. The bank burst into a hubbub of chatter and above me I could hear the old woman cackling away like a magpie. I finally worked my catch to the net and lifted it high out of water. A great roar of approval went up, and then together they all shouted something which, I later learned from Ben Swathmore, meant "Noble man."

The rainbow was almost six inches long.

〰〰〰Himself Was There

At least half a dozen different kinds of trout are recognized in Ireland, but if you'll stick to one kind of liquor, which no Irishman ever does, since he drinks whatever he can put his hands on, you'll find that the six or so are one, the brown. The problem of identity for the Irish icthyologist is a tough one, because the brown viewed through the umpteenth glass of Guinness is a very different fish from the brown seen through a bit of Jameson's. As for the local potato whiskey, it makes the brown downright dangerous, and you should not go near the stream without an ax in your hand. In any case, that is why they are called by different names, and a fine scheme it is too.

Not knowing what a marvelous country Ireland is for the angler, Sylvia and I frittered away much too much time in England and so had only a short time on the Emerald Isle— a bad mistake you should not repeat. Start your trip in Eire and you'll end there. An angler's dream it is. Seasons vary, but as a general rule you can fish for salmon from the first of the year to the end of September and the brown trout from February or March into October.

Our first whirl was for the salmon at Ballynahinch Castle in County Galway. The Ballynahinch River was developed by a very wealthy maharaja who wanted to get salmon in comfort, and this he did. There are seven beats on the stream, and a small rest house is placed at each one. So if the weather is bad, you can get out of the rain and have a pour without having every passing shepherd stop to find out how you're doing while he complains of the cold in his joints, with the end of his dry tongue lolling on his chest.

Much of the river is so narrow you can cast across it. You fish on well-constructed stone piers and walks, and there is nothing to interfere with your back casts, even though you are able to handle a long line. Near you stands a fine figure of a man with a net, your Irish ghillie. The antithesis of his Scotch counterpart, he agrees with everything you say.

"A fine day, Paul."

"Ah, yes sir, it is that indeed," he answers as he turns up his coat collar to keep the drizzle from running down his neck.

"Must be a salmon at the edge of that fast water."

"That's for sure, you'll be getting a hit now." This with great conviction, even though after forty years on the stream he's never heard of a salmon taking within thirty feet of the spot.

Don't let this disturb you; it's been going on since St. Patrick. The Irish are happy only if everyone else is too, so they have to do it this way. Occasionally the ghillie will volunteer some valuable information or ask an important question. "It's a good town this, three of the finest pubs in Ireland. Not far from here, either." Or, "Now had you noticed, sir, the fine taproom the castle has, all the choicest brands?"

As a matter of fact you had noticed it, and when you go back for lunch you should buy him a drink or two. And if he says "No," call the Dublin papers, because it will be the first time that that's happened in all of Ireland's history.

So Sylvia went shopping for tweeds while I fished the beautifully manicured Ballynahinch. Slow, deep pools, wide shallow weedy stretches, fast water tumbling blue-white over the stones. On two of the beats you can look back upstream to the castle with a lovely mountain rising behind it. Some of the river winds through green pasture with sheep and cattle grazing on either side, some of it is surrounded by trees and the rest by rhododendrons that the late maharaja had planted long ago.

First you fish with a fly, probably a Mar Lodge, and after that you change and go down through the water with a different pattern. You may repeat this half a dozen times. Finally you take your spinning rod and work it again with a spoon or an artificial minnow.

With good luck, Ballynahinch in the spring might give you one or two salmon a week. Later, the sea trout come into the river, and for my money they are just as much sport as the salmon if fished properly, on light trout tackle.

The Irish rods are likely to be even heavier and more awkward than the British— proper tackle for swordfish, but, unless you have the strength and desire to land your salmon by tossing it into the top of a tree, bring your own.

"Ah! And you have one," said my ghillie.

The salmon had followed a big silver spoon and had taken it right in front of me. He had taken much too close. One jump and he was free.

"Now that's a pity," sighed my ghillie. "A good fish, fifteen pounds for sure."

Ah, the Irish. A good people too, for sure. The fish didn't weigh ten and the ghillie knew it better than I.

An hour later, when we climbed the hill to the castle and made our way to the bar, the pretty young manageress asked us how we'd done.

"And a fine fish himself had on for a bit, close to twenty pounds," said my ghillie.

"Lamb for you tonight," added the young lady, "and no one's fault but your own."

I asked my ghillie if he'd have a spot of whiskey and he said, "Now I don't mind if I do, there being a bit of a chill in the air." He managed to get most of this in before I'd finished asking the question.

A while later, with the chill in the air coming under proper control, I glanced up to see a pile of tweeds walk into the room on a pair of female legs. The tweeds came to rest on a table top and Sylvia came out from behind them.

"Hah!" I said. "I see we are planning to open a store."

"They're marvelous. And they cost practically nothing. They must make them for fun." She looked at our drinks. "It's kind of chilly," she said.

"It's known as a bit of chill in the air," I informed her, "and Paul and I are busy dispelling it."

"I can see that. A bit more dispelling and you'll both fall in the river and drown." She turned to the barmaid. "A whiskey sour, please. And not another drop for them. As it is, they couldn't kill a salmon if they found it asleep on the bank."

As it developed, she was right and we didn't. But I worked at it. I must have changed flies twenty times that afternoon, but never a sign of a fish. It was a hopeless business, and finally we threw in the sponge and trudged back to the castle.

The next day Sylvia joined us at the top beat with her camera. She asked if she could try my two-handed seven-ounce Orvis rod for a few casts just to see if she could get the line out. She couldn't; she had a terrible time. The ghillie watched her make a couple of casts that were short of where the salmon lay by a good thirty feet. Since she obviously wasn't going to catch anything, he settled down on the ground, his back against a tree, and closed his eyes. I started straightening out my fly box.

"I've got one," she yelled.

I whirled around just in time to see it jump. It was a big salmon.

My ghillie came to life. "Quick, man, and help her. It's a great fish she has."

The fish came up again in a long powerful leap, then streaked downstream. The reel screamed and the rod looked like the rim of a wheel. And then the salmon broke. It is the only time I have ever seen a blood knot pull out. The day before I had tied about five feet of eight-pound-test nylon onto a heavy Hardy leader. The Hardy leader probably tested at least fourteen pounds, and the discrepancy between gut sizes apparently was too great. I made her a new leader and set up a rod for myself. But it didn't help. For us, that was the last salmon at Ballynahinch until we go back again.

It was pouring rain the next day when we took a thirty-mile bus trip to Ashford Castle, on Lough Corrib in County Mayo. We made only four stops on the run, not counting the stops to pick up or let off passengers. At each of the four there just happened to be a pub beside the bus, and at each of the four in went the driver, the conductor, and half the passengers. So the trip, though short in miles, takes a fair while to complete.

Ashford Castle is advertised as a "fairytale castle," and that it is, with modern plumbing, old oak-paneled public rooms, coats of arms, snapping log fires, excellent food, and all at the edge of the beautiful Lough Corrib.

This is a body of water two or three miles in width and thirty miles long. It is full of brown trout, a fair number of salmon, and pike, perch, bream, rudd, and char. The modest claim is made that this lough offers the best free fishing in the world, and it may be true. During the time we were there three salmon were taken, all on trout tackle.

The fairly accomplished fly fisherman will take more fish casting than trolling with artificial minnows. And have a lot more fun. In the off season— and April is considered that— the average is about three two-pound browns a day. You can come in empty-handed or you can get seven or eight. The largest brown caught while we were there weighed just over six pounds, but the all-time record for the lough is twenty-four. And sometimes, for a week or two between the middle of May and the middle of June, the mayfly is on the water and the dry-fly fisherman comes into his own, taking twenty, twenty-five fish a day. Or you can take to dapping. This is done with a special rod about sixteen feet long, a very light blow line that bellies out on the wind, a bit of leader, and a hook with several real mayflies impaled on it. The flies must ride right on top of the water, and you need a good wave to fish properly. When the trout or salmon takes he comes to the surface and draws in the flies as if he had all the time in the world. You count, "One dead trout, two dead trout, three dead trout," then strike. It is said to be good sport.

When you return in the evening, your fish are laid out in the castle tackle room along with all the others taken that day. The display is always impressive.

There are, they claim, three hundred and sixty-five islands in the lake, or one for every day of the year, all beautiful, and excellent places for picnic lunches.

My ghillie, a middle-aged Irishman named Johnny Gibbons, a fine chap and a fine storyteller, had been on Lough Corrib most of his life. When he discovered that I was a firm believer in leprechauns and fairies, we got along handsomely. While I cast over the shoals close by the islands, he told me tales of enchanted trout and kind fairies who come to people's aid. While I listened I sent my three tiny Irish flies on a 4X leader out over the waves and slowly retrieved. Johnny expertly maneuvered the boat with his oars and stopped talking only when we had to net a fish.

Sylvia went out on our last day with a young ghillie named Jack. She was trolling and we were to meet her at an island for lunch. After we'd been fishing a couple of hours our boat passed close to hers and I called, "Any luck?"

Her ghillie shouted, "Three," and held up three fingers.

"Ah, these young fellas are all liars," expounded Johnny. "Not a fish they've caught this morning." He was right, as it happened. But while we watched she caught her three, one right after the other. "And a kind fairy is watching over her," said Johnny. I agreed.

Sylvia's ghillie too knew that something was up, because after the third they caught no more. "It's a wrong I did you," he told her when they went in. "If I'd held up the fingers of both me hands, it's ten ye'd have in the boat for sure."

That evening, after dinner, we walked upstream along the bank of a broad river that flows beneath the castle bridge and into the lough. We came to the ruins of the ancient Abbey of

Cong, and to the little chapel-like house the monks built out over the river some hundreds of years ago. Here they used to fish for salmon of an evening, and there was a bench where they could sit as they worked their flies in the current below. An old drawing shows a shelf behind them where they kept their mugs of ale. And under the little structure there are the remains of a trap so ingeniously designed that if a fish got caught his struggles set a bell to ringing in the distant abbey kitchen and the cook put salmon on the menu for that night.

Alas, the salmon no longer pause at that lovely spot, for time and floods have scoured the lies away. But standing by the little ruined house, it is not hard to see those fine monks who, stone by stone, built one of the world's greatest abbeys, resting their tired limbs, their long rods in one hand and their good Irish ale in the other. And sure and the kind fairies watch over the spot now, and no good will come to you if you lay a fly there.

~~~The Pawnbroker

Back in the 1890's, so the story goes, three brothers from New York City, the Wallaces, joined a Quebec fishing club. Frank, Peter, and Ralph were pawnbrokers, and everything the two older brothers touched turned into platinum. By the time Frank, the eldest and the founder of the business, reached sixty they were in somewhat better shape than Fort Knox. Ralph, just turned thirty (the product of a younger stepmother), did not see the compulsion for sweating it out to acquire still more millions. Unlike his much older brothers, he had not started out in a hole in the wall with overdue rent. By the time he was old enough to tell the top from the bottom he was ensconced in Groton. From there he went to Princeton, where he lasted just six months, until a Princeton yard cop found him in bed with one of the deans' wives. At that point— he was nineteen— it seemed like a logical time to retire and to devote the rest of his life to fly fishing and the pursuit of ladies, and this he did.

Frank and Peter both enjoyed their two weeks a year of trout fishing at the Ignatius Club forty miles north of Quebec City. But for Ralph it was a way of life. While the elder Wallaces and the other club members were fond of the happy-go-lucky, poverty-stricken, priest-dominated little town of St. Albans, for Ralph the town had everything to offer that New York lacked, including no street cars, excellent fishing and hunting, and, to his way of thinking, much prettier and easier-to-come-by women. At the age of thirty, just divorced from his third chorus girl, Ralph announced that he was retiring to St. Albans.

At that time there were no television sets, and St. Albans, like hundreds of other small Quebec hamlets, was run by the parish priest. If an unmarried girl got pregnant she went to hell, if a married woman committed adultery she went there too, and the same for a man. If a family moved to a larger town, or worse, to the States, they all went to hell. If anyone learned to speak English he or she was bound for down under, and if you skipped the sermon and confession on Sunday you were doomed. And if you wanted to stay out of the fiery hereafter, ten percent of every dollar you earned went into the coffers of the church. It was your job to be a lumberjack or a guide, get as drunk as you pleased on occasions, keep your wife pregnant and leave the other ladies alone. That was about all the Lord asked of you.

The village doctor, a kindly intelligent man, performed a vast number of abortions on the town's unwed and secretly advised at least ninety percent of the males about a certain address in Quebec City where illegal birth-control devices could be had, just in case they wanted to do a little experimenting outside the home. But not at home— the doctor like the priest was of the firm belief that God wanted the Catholics to take over the world and the quickest way to accomplish this was for every wife to produce ten or a dozen kids. Unknown to the priest, whom they all adored, no girl had gone to the altar to say "I will" as a virgin for the last seven years, and no one in the town other than the doctor had ever gone beyond the eighth grade.

Then Ralph came to town and carried on in broad daylight as the others had done in the depths of the forest or under cover of darkness. Ralph was not a Catholic. Indeed, Ralph had not been near any kind of church since escaping Groton's required chapel services.

Ralph hit the town of St. Albans with the impact of a fly swatter on a bug. The payoff was when he purchased a beautiful horsedrawn hearse that moved on wheels in summer and runners in winter. With the uniformed coachman on the box and four lively horses in front Ralph would charge up and down through the town, stretched out on an innerspring mattress with the lady of the moment in his arms. The two of them, when not intertwined, would gaze out of the big curtainless windows and wave at the grinning populace. Ralph couldn't care less who saw what, and that included his holy nibs, the priest. His idea was that life was created to be enjoyed to the full, and the village priest could stick his head in the pond and see if he cared.

While Ralph and his brothers had far more than their share of the world's wealth, there was a good deal of questioning among the members as to how they had gotten into the Ignatius Club in the first place— something to do with Ralph's being an old Grotonian. But once the mistake had been made, if mistake it was, no one really regretted it. They were jolly characters, and they did add a good deal of *joie de vivre* to what otherwise might, on occasions, have been a slightly stuffy organization. And all three were excellent fly fishermen who returned to the water the fish they did not want to eat.

So Ralph in his horsedrawn hearse with the clear sides raced all over town and past the church, even on Sunday mornings when the bells were tolling for Mass. His many sleigh bells made far more noise than the antiquated old bell on the church steeple.

Father Cheval was aware that his flock was being led down the wrong alley and that if this sort of business continued the younger members of his parish might start commiting some of those sins— God forbid— that they had all been up to for years behind his back. But how to stop it? The holy father realized that this heathen, Ralph Wallace, was a law unto himself. Father Cheval could understand this well, because he boasted an identical legal status. While he was vaguely aware that a million miles away in a place called Rome there was a Vatican, he was rather confused as to just what the Vatican consisted of or what his relationship was to the Pope. Father Cheval, too, had once been a lumberjack, and, like most small remote Quebec hamlet priests, had the barest essentials of an education. He could conduct a wedding, funeral, or Mass largely in Latin even though he didn't have the faintest idea what the words meant. But what was important was that Father Cheval stuck to his job of keeping the wives pregnant and doubled and redoubled the town's population as if the inhabitants were fruit flies.

No one had ever told Father Cheval that the best defense is an attack— he worked that one out in his wise old head. He called together twenty of St. Alban's toughest young lumberjacks and talked to them about hell and evil and what was going to happen to everyone in town if the devil's representative, Ralph Wallace, was not driven out of the town, out of the county, and out of La Belle Province de Quebec into the lands of evil that had spawned him. The lumberjacks took their religion, like their drinking and their sex, seriously. They loved their priest, whom they were counting on to get them into heaven in spite of their sins, and they were deeply moved. And they were acutely aware that Ralph Wallace was taking too many of the town's pretty young girls out of circulation. So when Father Cheval concluded by announcing that next Tuesday night he wanted them to march on Ralph Wallace's villa and burn it to the ground, release the horses from the stables, then burn the stables too, they were for him to a man. In fact, it sounded like a splendid party. They were told that afterward they could all gather at the St. Albans Lodge and he would see to it that the drinks were on the house.

Father Cheval made a few mistakes. He should have settled on half a dozen men, not twenty. And he should have included one older man among them and put him in charge, though as things turned out the late Charles de Gaulle never could have controlled that mob. And he should have announced the fire the day of the fire, not three days ahead.

The trouble started when one of the jacks got drunk on Sunday and confided in a blond lady who, he had good reason to believe, was loyal to him. He didn't know it but five days before she'd had her first ride in the hearse and was slated for her fourth ride on the morrow. Once her regular escort passed out, the lady lost no time in beating it to Ralph's huge architectural monstrosity on his private lake, where he divided his time between fishing and various beds. Ralph listened to the blonde, then gave her a kiss and a drink. As he contemplated the problem a wide grin spread from one ear to the other.

At eight p.m. on Tuesday the twenty lumberjacks arrived on schedule, each man equipped with a blazing torch and a couple of whiskeys under the belt, to right the wrongs of their beloved priest. And to get some of the town's cuties back into circulation. They sang a ribald song of the lumber camps as they marched four abreast down the winding replica of a Venetian palace entrance to a French Canadian builder's idea of a seventeenth-century Italian villa, complete with moat and swans.

As they neared the house they suddenly found themselves in a blaze of outdoor lights. The huge studded doors swung open and out danced twenty ladies of the night, imported at an awful price from Quebec, and attired in scanty panties and see-through bras that left the barest modicum to their lumberjack imaginations. And each dancing lady was equipped with a whiskey bottle. From inside could be heard the sound of a banjo and a fiddle.

"Come on in, boys, and have a few drinks and some fun before you burn us down. The fire will keep, but the fun won't," bellowed a generously curved blonde. She threw her arms around a jack and gave him a long kiss. "Throw your torches in the drive. We'll get you some matches to light 'em later."

The crowd of arsonists halted in its tracks as each member studied the females and all that unconsumed booze. "Why not?" shouted a husky bearded jack. "We can burn the damn place any time. Who's to stop us? Come on, girlie." He threw his arm around a redhead and they jigged inside.

These girlies of *le soir* had not been recruited from the campus of La Salle University. They might be young and pretty, but that didn't mean they didn't know how to handle a bunch of lumberjacks five times as strong as they were. Within an hour's time half a dozen of the jacks were sleeping quietly under tables.

Ralph Wallace now appeared to make a speech. His eyes filled with tears as he told how his life had been one of evil and how before he died (he was as strong as an ox but at this point he had a fit of coughing and stumbled as if about to fold up and expire on the spot) he wanted to make peace with his creator and set things to rights. The lumberjacks who were still upright, each with a girl on his lap, promptly made up their minds that Ralph Wallace was a pretty fine fellow after all and there was nothing they wouldn't do for him, just as long as it didn't conflict with the interests of Father Cheval. They squeezed their ladies, had another drink, and toasted, "Long live Ralph Wallace." The ladies all joined in. After all, not one of them had ever made this much money before in twenty-four hours. And up to now there had been no serious wear and tear on their chassis.

"And so," Ralph lamented in funereal tones, "Here we all live in God's chosen spot— no such beautiful town anywhere. And no nobler man of God on earth than your own beloved Father Duval." There was a loud cheer. The fact that he had gotten the priest's name wrong at this hour bothered no one.

"Look at this beautiful home." Ralph waved an arm. "And what do we have for a church? That fallen-down wreck of a building a cow would be ashamed to calve in. My friends, this town needs a new church, a church worthy of Father Buval and his devotion to the Lord. If that church happened to burn to the ground, I know it's insured to the top of the steeple. And if it happens to burn this night I promise that I will add enough to the insurance to erect, not another church, but a cathedral. And with two bell towers, and large enough so that only one Mass will be needed instead of three. And the same with the sermons. Father Whatchamacallum is not a young man any longer, and he shouldn't have to do all that work."

Ralph paused until the thunder of applause died. "Now I'll pick four men to do the job," he said. "And there's something else if you burn that church to the ground. Father Googal gets lifetime rights to fish my private lake. For your information, it's stocked with four- and five-pound brookies."

Another yell went up. To a man they knew how much Father Cheval loved to fish. They knew well enough so that when they lured the St. Albans maidens into the bush they always stayed well away from the streams.

Ralph picked the four most enthusiastic jacks and sent them on their way, first assuring them that the party would just be getting started when they returned.

In his small house near the church, Father Cheval slept in peace. He wore a wide beatific smile as he dreamed beautiful dreams of the flames crackling through that heathen's villa. In fact, the crackling of flames finally woke him. A quarter of a second later he was out of bed and at the window gazing on the holocaust. The flames were fifty feet in the air and the St. Albans volunteer fire department's hand-drawn pump couldn't have saved a door knob, even had it been there, which it wasn't. At the time the fire department was enjoying Ralph's luxuries.

Father Cheval knelt and prayed. He realized that he was doomed, because Father Cheval possessed knowledge that Ralph and those wretched jacks did not. There was no fire insurance and hadn't been since the father, a priest a bit ahead of his time, had taken on a young dentist's widow in Quebec and set her up in a small house on the outskirts well removed

from neighbors where his comings and goings would not be noted.

The holy father did the best he could. He broke down the following day and confessed all to Ralph Wallace. Ralph swallowed hard and told him not to worry.

The two-spire cathedral was erected with such bells as you couldn't believe. On a clear day they can be heard in the next town, eight miles away. When they ring, Ralph orders his coachman to stop the hearse while he and the lady with him cross themselves. And the dentist's widow now frequently pays long visits to Ralph's home so that she and Father Cheval can fish and commune together.

🌊🌊🌊Wanda

My nephew, Euripides Montezuma Warner, was named that way because my brother's wife was a firm believer in the prenatal influence of names. She was undecided as to whether she would be content with another Eugene O'Neill . . . "What a play! I hear he's going to get the Nobel Prize. Oh, look at that gorgeous creature dripping diamonds. That's his mother. All his talent comes from that side." Or should she move to Mexico and produce him there . . . white ermine robe and a scepter. "Such a kindly ruler, the people adore him. And the queen mother . . ." she wondered how rubies would look in her crown.

Unfortunately, at the age of four, just after he climbed out of diapers, his Uncle Robert, guiding his little hand, managed to get Euripides attached to a trout by dropping a dry fly on a pool, and any prenatal influence there might have been was wiped out clean as a snake's tonsils. His little die was cast; he was going to be a fisherman. Three days later he proved it by making it on his own. He caught all the tropical fish in his father's library tank, one of which was very rare and had cost a hundred and fifteen dollars.

Rip, as he was called, was turned bottom side up and got the treatment. Deter him? Not at all, this boy was on his way. The next day, with his anatomy too sore to sit on, he found some white grubs and slaughtered all the goldfish in the little pool in front of the house. I have heard it said that when a man thinks of heaven as a place where he is attached to a large salmon on a perfect river instead of being spread out on a sofa with a blond nymphomaniac he is showing his years. If so, Rip started showing his at four, and he attained twenty-eight without giving a girl a second glance or a polite word. Fish, yes, girls no. NO in caps.

Sylvia and I asked Rip to accompany us on a land-locked-salmon trip to Lake Winnipesaukee in New Hampshire, and he accepted with the interest a starving tiger would show in twenty pounds of raw meat.

Everything was perfect until the day we left, when a girl named Wanda, the daughter of Sylvia's ex-roommate at Wells, fresh out of Buenos Aires, turned up with a note from her ma asking Sylvia if we could put her up for a while. She had never been out of Argentina before.

Young Wanda was some dish. If she had belonged to me I would have chloroformed her and had her stuffed. She was the absolute pinnacle of what a female can become, and all of it in just twenty-two years. I was fifty-six at the time and when I first saw her my heart stopped beating for at least ten minutes.

"Wanda, have you ever been on a fishing trip?" asked Sylvia.

Rip made a noise like a wounded Cape buffalo about to charge from ten feet.

"Only once or twice. Sounds like fun." She laughed. I gave up breathing.

Noise from the other side of the room like a man going down for the third time.

My eternally matchmaking wife said that we had to run downtown to do some shopping and suggested that Wanda and Rip go for a swim in the pool.

"Can't," Rip said. "Waiting for a long-distance call."

Sylvia looked at him as if he'd fallen out of the chimney, then said, "Bob, if you want anything to drink on this trip you'd better go buy it. Come on, Wanda, let's go swimming."

So Rip stomped upstairs, growling and swearing as he went. I finally managed to ease my eyes back into their sockets, murmured something about seeing them shortly, and drove ninety miles an hour to town to get the booze. Even though I too am something of a piscatorial addict I was beginning to think that Rip was hardly worth saving. Twenty-eight, unattached, a fine fly fisherman but no brains, and with an opportunity like this dropped kerplunk on his doorstep. And I remembered Sylvia telling me that her ex-roommate, Wanda Senior, and her husband were both up to their hips in chips. How could this dummy miss?

The next day we flew to Concord, New Hampshire, and Wanda, with all male eyes upon her except the ones that should have been, sat next to Rip and tried to make conversation. She would have done better if she'd tried to chat with a Central Park statue. Rip was reading a book on fishing. All she got out of him were snorts and grunts.

Sylvia leaned forward. "Wanda, have you ever fly-fished?" she asked.

Rip snorted.

Wanda blushed. "Yes, a little with my father."

Rip looked at her. "Ha!" he said. He could tell she was lying.

We got a U-Drive-It in Concord and headed for Christmas Tree Island on Winnipesaukee. The island had an excellent motel and restaurant. Since we had only two rooms, I had to share one with my scintillating nephew, who continued to grunt and snort around with all the charm of a wild boar rooting for acorns. This, I thought, sure promised to be a wonderful trip.

Over drinks by the lake shore, Sylvia said, "Rip can lend you a rod, Wanda. He always has lots of tackle. Why don't you two fish together tomorrow? We'll meet here for dinner."

"Haven't a rod the right weight for her. Maybe Bob can lend her one, if he doesn't mind having it busted. Why not cut a twig and tie a string on it?"

"I have a four-ounce Orvis rod and a six line. Just right for you. Don't worry," I said, trying to bail the poor girl out.

"You two better take her in the boat. I'm going to wade the river," said my bursting-with-politeness nephew.

"Oh, wading sounds like sport. That's the way Daddy fishes. Don't worry, I'll stay well out of your way."

So in spite of a behavior pattern that would have driven a lesser lady right up the wall, the next morning Rip and Wanda took the car and drove off for the river while Sylvia and I and a guide trolled flies from a boat. I caught one two-pound salmon and that was it for the day. At four p.m. Sylvia suggested that we go in. "Poor girl, she's probably sitting there in a pool of tears. I could gladly skin that nephew of yours."

"He's an ass," I said. "No hope for him. My fault. I never should have taken him fishing when he was a baby."

Sylvia nodded. "Right. You should have drowned him."

They were not back at four and they were not back at seven. Darkness began to descend. At eight-thirty Sylvia said, "Perhaps we ought to call the police."

At that moment they drove in and parked by the motel. We heard gales of happy laughter.

"My God!" murmured Sylvia.

Then I saw them. He was carrying two huge landlocks. Both were over eight pounds.

Sylvia and I have been fishing Winnipesaukee for fifteen years and neither of us has ever taken a fish of eight pounds.

"Where in heaven's name did you get those, Rip?" I asked.

He dropped a fish on the lawn and put his free arm around Wanda's waist. "I didn't. Didn't catch a damn thing. Wanda got 'em, and a lot of little four- and five-pounders she threw back. On a nymph. What a girl! Whoever would have thought of that?" He squeezed her. "Unfortunately she sprained her wrist landing that big one— just eleven pounds— so she can't fish any more. She's going to have to get that wrist X-rayed and taped up. It's all swollen."

Sylvia looked first at Wanda, then at Rip.

Rip said, "Let's go back to Concord tomorrow. This girl needs to see a doctor. I'm afraid she's going to have to wear a sling. Why don't we all go back home tomorrow? No fun sitting around a fishing camp with your arm in a sling."

Sylvia looked at him again, then at Wanda.

"Gosh!" Rip said. "A nymph. Who would have ever thought of it?" His arm went around her again. "Except you."

In the office of the country doctor the next morning, Wanda told him and Sylvia all. The confession followed the doctor's remark, "I can't figure it out. That wrist doesn't look as if you fell on it. Looks more like you pounded it with a stick."

Wanda had never cast in her life, she told the doctor. She had just watched her father. She had tried casting well below and out of sight of Rip, but it didn't work. Finally she gave up and tried to find Rip. No luck. So she just sat on the bank and cried and cried. And while she was sitting there in her pool of tears, who should come along but kindly old Frank Davis, Director of Fish and Game for New Hampshire. She told him all, including how mean Rip was and how, in spite of it all, she thought perhaps she loved him. She wished she was dead. Frank took her by the hand and pulled her to her feet. He handed her a large handkerchief and said, "Blow. We're going to teach that young man a lesson."

A five-mile drive in his car brought them to a state hatchery where they were netting and killing brooder salmon to test for mercury content. Frank picked out the two largest and threw them in the car. "Now, let me see . . . yuh! I got it. You caught 'em on a nymph. Your dad gave you a few in Argentina." He fished four out of a fly box in the car's glove compartment. "Now we got a problem. Tomorrow this kid is going to want to see you perform. Hmm! Like this boy enough to sprain your wrist?"

She nodded. "Yes."

"Okay, when we get back to the stream I'll cut you a stick. You grit your teeth and sock that wrist hard. Hit it several times, till it starts to swell. Then you'll have to quit fishing for several days."

"Oh!" she said. "You're marvelous." She leaned across and kissed him.

The country doctor broke out laughing. "You know you damned near broke that wrist. Think I'll put it in a splint. We'll tell him you fractured a bone." He looked at her. "But

what happens when you take the splint off? When he wants to take you fishing again?"

She smiled. "Mr. Davis has that all worked out too. I'm going to visit a friend. What I'm really going to do is go to Manchester, Vermont, to a fly-fishing school. Mr. Davis says if I work hard for two weeks I'll look like an expert. And he's given me a list of books to read in the evenings."

Five weeks later, when we went fishing again, Wanda could handle seventy feet of line with a three-and-a-half-ounce rod and she looked just like the how-to-do-it pictures of the men in the books.

Happily Wanda's parents came to the United States for the wedding, so we didn't all have to go to Buenos Aires.

When the reception line finally broke up, Rip whispered, "Say, who was that old geezer who put his arms round you and kissed you?"

"Frank Davis. He's a friend of Daddy's. I think he runs a mill or something."

Five years after the wedding, Sylvia told me the story of the big landlocks. I don't think Rip knows yet, but they have two kids and he's so much in love I doubt it would make any difference now. Why, she even persuaded him to take a job, something all the family put together couldn't even approach. He's a park ranger in Vermont, close by the Batten Kill, finest trout river in the East.

ᔋᔋᔋThe Last Salmon

One Atlantic salmon of over sixty pounds and one just under have been taken on flies from Norway's Lars River. A number of years ago I leased this river for a week.

The fish were not taking well, and, to make matters worse, I suspected that I had come down with the grippe. Later I learned that what I had come down with was TB, but even if I had been aware of it at the time I would have kept right on fishing. Good salmon water in Norway is expensive and not easy to come by. So with a temperature that never dropped under a hundred, I fished each of the seven days, except the last, from early morning until cocktail time. On my last day I quit at noon.

My ghillie, Olaf, was very old, close to eighty. He was huge, at least six and a half feet tall. He moved slowly, stooped over like a great bear. Olaf was a quiet man. When I waded he

would crouch on the shore with his enormous gnarled hands resting on his knees, the long gaff in front of him. He seldom spoke.

There was just one pool we fished by boat, known as Upper Pool. It was about two hundred and fifty yards long and a couple of hundred feet wide. Above it, white water tumbled down a long rapids, and at the bottom the pool ended with a low fall and another set of rapids. Olaf maneuvered the boat so that my fly covered every square yard of the water. He had been a Lars ghillie since his fifteenth down and he knew his business.

I was aware that he did not approve of my six-ounce Orvis fly rod, that he considered it much too light for the work at hand. Even after I managed to take a twenty-four-pound salmon he shook his head. "The salmon, sometimes they are very big. Maybe you will see." Another shake of his head. "Your rod is too little."

The twenty-four-pounder was the only fish I had landed by the final day. On that day we fished the Upper Pool. We started at the top and worked slowly down and back and forth. At the end of the first hour Olaf said, "I think maybe you should try a Jock Scott, the biggest one you have."

He held the boat against the current while I tied on the fly. On my first cast a salmon took. As it did not jump I had no idea of its size. Then it went downstream, almost the length of the pool. It swam with tremendous power and speed. I was sure that it was going over the falls and into the fast water where it would be impossible for us to follow, as the rapids ran through a gorge and the water was much too fast and heavy for a boat. But the salmon stopped a couple of yards above the fast water and lay there, heavy as a log.

Les Gordon, the Orvis rod maker, once told me that if I

could ever break one of his rods on a fish, no matter how light the rod or heavy the fish, he would give me a new one. I thought this was going to be the day I was going to collect. With the drag on the reel screwed all the way down I gripped the two-handed butt and hauled back until I thought my arms were coming out of their sockets. Finally the salmon moved and came back upstream and went past us straight up into the fast water for nearly fifty yards.

"I see his back. A big fish, a very big one," Olaf said.

In time we got the salmon back into the pool. I had had him on for nearly an hour when he began to tire.

Olaf rowed the boat to the center of the pool and beached it. "You get out," he said. "I gaff him here."

I still had not seen the salmon, and it was another ten minutes before I worked it into shallow water and finally did see it. It was enormous.

The fish rolled on its side, then made a feeble effort to get back into deep water. It was only a yard from the bank. The old man, stooped over, gaff in hand, waded into the pool and slid the hook of the gaff across the salmon's back. As he jerked the gaff toward him to drive the point home he suddenly fell headlong, across the fish and into deep water.

Things happened so fast I can hardly remember their order. My leader broke. Whether I pulled too hard or Olaf snapped it as he fell I do not know. There was a gigantic splash as the fish came back to life and broke out from under the old man. I dropped my rod and waded in to help him get ashore.

He was soaking wet and his hands were shaking. His eyes filled with tears. "I lose your fish. I am too old. I never fish again. I lose your fish." He began to sob.

A couple of months later, in a New York hospital with my TB, I learned that he had died a few weeks after I had left the river. The owner of the Lars wrote that Olaf had never gone back to the river again. Indeed, from the day he lost the fish he had never stepped out of his house again. How big was that salmon? Olaf said that it was over twenty kilos, or forty-four pounds. It seemed all of that to me. Anyway, it was a tough one to lose, and tougher for Olaf than for me, for no matter how old he is the Norwegian ghillie, like his Scotch, Irish, and Canadian counterparts, hates the day when finally he must leave the river. For men like Olaf there is not much point to life after that.

*⌗⌗⌗*To Make Crime Pay

About a dozen years ago, Don Jarden, an old friend and a senior editor of the *National Geographic,* called me long-distance. He said, "We're getting out a new edition of our book on the world's fishes. I need some pictures of big brookies, four pounds up, caught in the U. S. Have you got any?"

"Sure. Lots of them."

"That's wonderful. Send 'em by air mail, we're about to go to press. I'll call you about the price once I see them."

"Just one problem," I said. "Of course it doesn't make any difference, but none of the trout were caught in the U. S. They were all taken in Quebec."

"We can't use them. This is a U. S. trout story. Trout have to be caught here."

"What the hell!" I said. "Who's going to know?"

There was a long pause, then Don, in a voice that would

have chilled an erupting volcano, said, "You and I would know."

So that was that. Temporarily I gave up a life of crime, largely, I guess, because no opportunities came my way.

Then, some years later, I went tarpon fishing on the Keys in Florida with a wonderful guy named Jerry Bickford. Jerry, the president of one of the country's largest engineering firms, was as excited as a six-year-old because he'd met an outdoor-magazine editor at dinner who had agreed to buy a tarpon story if he could send in a picture of a fish of over one hundred pounds. "Keys are loaded with big tarpon this time of year," Jerry said. "It's going to be a cinch."

But it wasn't. There were ten people in the camp, us included, but no one could budge a tarpon. We cast flies and plugs, trolled, the works, but not a tarpon. Jerry was as depressed as if he'd had a contract to build a new bridge across the Hudson canceled. You would have thought his life depended on seeing his name in an outdoor magazine.

Then, on our last day, I got a tarpon. It wasn't exactly a hundred pounds— in fact it was just six— but at least it was a tarpon.

Jerry studied the little fish for a long time, then a happy grin went from one ear to the other. "I've got it!" he shouted. "But keep that tarpon wet. If the skin dries out it won't work. Now I have to think."

He thought out loud all through two martinis and lunch. By the time he'd polished off a demitasse everything was worked out. His enthusiasm accounted for a louder than normal voice. The other eight guests were now all in the act, all bent on getting him into that outdoor magazine with a color shot of someone connected to a hundred-pound fish.

I suggested we go to Ringling Brothers' winter quarters in

Sarasota and rent the smallest midget in the joint to hold up the tarpon.

Jerry shook his head. "Nope. Editor could tell it was a midget from a mile off. Leave this deal to me. Hey, you got a wide-angle lens?"

I didn't, but the guy at the far corner table did, a Nikon lens that would fit Jerry's camera. This chap's wife, a real rarity in Florida because she is one of the handful of people who were born there, spoke up: "Mah! You all are shoah goin' to a lot o' trouble to photograph that poah little fish. Ahm comin' daown to watch."

And she did, along with everyone else in the camp.

Jerry was all efficiency. He set his camera up on a tripod, explaining, "We'll put the boat there. And the fish will jump here." Then he went into a lot of technical gobbledegook about how he needed the tripod because he had to take his pictures at a rather slow speed with the smallest lens aperture possible so he would get what he called depth of field, in other words everything in focus from the foreground to the skyline. It all sounded pretty complicated, but since he was an M. I. T. graduate I hoped he knew what he was doing.

Our audience, the other eight guests plus a few grizzled Florida guides, sat in a row of chairs along the beach to watch. Jerry was all business. "Now let me see. Hey, you there with the long hair, go get a stout pole and six feet of strong string. You, Bob, wake up and get off the beach. You're the fisherman. Wade out to that outboard. Wait a minute, take your rod. Joe, get that boat in closer to shore and anchor it bow and aft alongside the beach. Make sure your anchor ropes don't show."

One of the bystanders brought down Scotch, soda, and a pailful of ice for the audience. "Hey, Bob, want a drink?" he called.

"Of course," I shouted back.

"No," said Jerry. "He's working. I'm not going to have him landing a tarpon with a highball in his hand." Then he turned to his Florida assistants. "One of you guys find a rock. Get a big one. We have to tie his line"— pointing to me— "around it so he'll look as though he had a fish on."

A kid brought a jagged stone he could hardly lift. Jerry wrapped my leader around it three times and tied a knot, then he waded out and dropped the rock halfway between the shore and the boat. I shouted, "Testing," and leaned back on the rod. Everything held. A cheer went up from the bleachers.

Next Jerry took off one of his socks and filled it with sand. He tied it to the end of a string, and tied the other end of the string to a pole. "Now," he explained to his assistants, "when I shout 'Go,' pull this sock out of the water and over your head, out of the picture. This makes the splash for the jumping fish. At the same time, Pete, you lift the tarpon out of the water, dripping wet, and toss it straight up over the splash made by the sock so it will look like a tarpon jumping. And don't get your hands in the picture. Ready? Hey, Bob, lean back on that rod and look desperate. Remember you're playing a hundred-pound fish. All set? Go!"

The tarpon jumped tail first and got tangled up with the sock. There was laughter and booing from the audience.

"Terrible," Jerry shouted. "Pete, the tarpon comes out of water head first, not ass backwards— excuse me, ladies. Practice till you get it right."

Pete threw the tarpon a dozen times and each time retrieved it in the knee-deep water. Finally he had it. "Now, when I shout 'Go,'" boomed Jerry, "you wait, Pete, till the sock is on the way out of the picture, then throw the fish."

"Ready? Go!

"That was better, but the sock was still in the picture. Bob,

show some excitement. You look as if you were walking in your sleep."

After thirty-six exposures Jerry put in a new roll of film. Our audience had all departed except the young Florida wife. When Jerry finished his third roll of thirty-six exposures and had started to put in a new one, she shook her head and said, "Ye know as lawng as ah live ah'm nevah goin' believe any-thin' ah read owah see agin," and she departed.

I saw Jerry two weeks later at lunch in New York and he showed me two color slides. "Perfect," he said modestly.

I held them up to the light. They were that. There was I, leaning back, my glass fly rod bent like a horseshoe, and there was the leaping tarpon in front of me, about ten feet before the camera. That six-pound fish looked a lot more like two hundred pounds than one.

"Boy, wait till they see this," said Jerry. "In the story I tell about you landing a hundred-and-sixty-pound fish on a fly. If I'd made it much bigger you would have been nudging the world's record and the editor might get suspicious."

A month later I saw Jerry again. "Did you sell the story?" I asked.

He looked at me and shook his head sadly. Then he pulled a letter out of his pocket. I read it.

"Dear Mr. Bickford, We are returning your story, 'Record Tarpon,' and the two color slides of the jumping fish. If that tarpon had weighed 160 pounds I doubt very much that the fisherman would have had the line wrapped around his finger. If the fish had cut the finger in two, as it would have done if it had been real, and if the end of the finger had been floating free, I would have bought it. As it is, sorry, we don't run fakes."

"Hell!" I said. "What a dumb mistake."

Jerry looked at me and shook his head. "You're telling me!"

ᴓᴓᴓ Le Champion

The St. Bernard Fish & Game Club, or what little is left of it, celebrated its hundredth anniversary in 1972, making it the oldest fishing club in La Belle Province, if not in the whole of Canada. During most of the twenty-five years that I have been a member we have had five hundred square miles of forests, rivers, and lakes under lease, ample water for our eighty members to fish, from our largest lake, ten miles in length, to well over one hundred and fifty smaller lakes and ponds. There was a saying at the club that if the trout weren't taking you didn't change flies, you just changed lakes.

George Mixter, an elderly Boston scholar and a thoroughly delightful person, was once asked to write the club's history. George promptly rounded up our oldest and most articulate guide, Jules Frappier, a little French Canadian in his eighties who was as fine a raconteur as he was a woodsman. George spent many hours listening to Jules' tales of long-ago days and taking them all down as Jules talked. The tales were wonderful and George was sure he had struck gold until he noticed, reviewing his notes, one or two small discrepancies. So he rounded up Jules again, and once more Jules, in broken English, recounted all the old stories.

At that point, George, with a learned man's insistence on accuracy, gave up the history, because on the second go-around Jules' tales had all improved. The hungry wolves which had followed him across the frozen lake in the 1890's the first time had numbered six, the second time there were twenty-two. The crazed bear that the first time had charged him and put him up a tree and almost gotten his foot, the second time had gotten him by the foot, and Jules had had to unlace his boot so the bear could pull it off, allowing him to climb up to safety in his sock. And so it went with every anecdote. Jules would have made an excellent speaker for a Kiwanis or Rotary Club dinner but a poor candidate for a Ph.D. in history.

As the years passed, Jules, who weighed only a hundred and twenty pounds, found the canoes heavier to carry over the trails. The club's officers suggested that he hang up his shield and accept a small pension— after all he was eighty-two— but Jules would have none of it. He would pound his chest and claim that he could out-walk, out-paddle, and out-perform any other guide in the country and that he was as tough now as sixty years ago, so let there be no chatter about his quitting. When it was time to retire he would let them know.

Jules continued guiding, and the officers arranged for him to be assigned to new members or guests who did not know the property. Because Jules had now slowed down to the point where the only lakes and ponds— a very small minority— that he would recommend trying were those within a hundred yards of a road. For him, at last, the canoes had put on weight.

In the summer of 1957, Jules was drowned. Had a canoe overturned in a storm it might have been a fitting end for a fine old man who had spent his life in the wilderness and had become almost legendary— even James Oliver Curwood, once a guest at the club, had devoted several pages to the incredible Jules. But no, Jules had not had a noble ending, he had drowned in twelve inches of water.

Once a month Jules received an old-age relief check from Ottawa, and this was always immediately cashed in the town's only bar, the St. Andrews Lodge, and Jules would proceed to get drunk and stay drunk until his money was all spent. So at one a.m. on a Friday morning, Jules, having consumed his final nickel's worth of booze, put on his lumber jacket and on his third attempt managed to negotiate the door and stagger out into a heavy snowfall. Foolishly, he decided to leave the main road and take a short cut across the fields to his home, a one-room tarpaper-covered shack with a wood stove and no running water, where he dwelt alone.

It was the broom factory that was his undoing. Instead of walking around the small circular pond used to soak lumber, he chose to cross it on the foot-wide path that bisected it, perhaps as proof to himself that he was soberer than some people might think. That morning when the mill opened, Jules was found face down in the pond. He had not gotten a yard from shore before he went off the plank.

Whether he had had a heart attack or the shock of the cold water had killed him no one knew. In any case there was not a bruise on him, so he had not struck anything in his fall.

His funeral was one of the largest ever held in the St.

Andrews Catholic church. Jules had been related to about half the town. He had been one of fourteen children, nine of whom survived him; there were children, grandchildren, and great-grandchildren, nephews and nieces and their children, first, second, and third cousins. In addition to all of these, the club's twelve directors and four officers were in the church, plus a number of the older members. There were board chairmen and banking, insurance, and manufacturing presidents, all for a little French Canadian who had never learned to read or write, but still a man who knew how to paddle with the best of them, who could fiddle or dance all night long, and whose endless tales of the bygone days were reminiscent of Paul Bunyan's adventures but had a ring of truth to them which the picturesque Bunyan stories often did not.

There are so many tales about Jules Frappier, most of them bearing at least a modicum of the truth, that it is hard to select just one to remember him by. I am sure that if the fifty-odd club members who knew him well were to choose fifty stories as representative of his past, no two tales would be the same. How any one man dwelling in that backwoods forgotten little town of St. Andrews could have become involved in so many harrowing adventures in eighty-three years of life none of us will ever know. But he did.

In St. Andrews the favorite sport is neither hunting nor fishing, which the male population, made up in its entirety of born poachers, takes for granted; no indeed, it is racing trotters, and has been for two hundred years. Every man in town rich enough to own a second- or third-hand car also owns a sulky and a horse. And no matter how a man's wife and ten or more kids may fare, the trotter eats and dwells as if owned by a Saratoga millionaire. The town has no movie, poolroom, bowling alley, or dance hall, but it does have a well-kept mile-

and-a-quarter track and a grandstand large enough to seat the village.

There are races every Saturday when snow is off the ground, but the great annual event is held the first Saturday in August. A generous purse is provided from the men's lumberjacking and guiding wages, and foreign horses, from as far away as Shawinigan Falls and Trois-Rivières, are invited to compete. By one-thirty, back in 1902, when Jules Frappier let go on an ancient tuneless bugle found in a Louisville trash can to announce the first race, nine-tenths of the men in the stands over sixteen, the town's doctor and two Catholic priests excepted, were full of booze. And half the women were only a drink or two behind.

On this particular August day the affair fell far below expectations because the Trois-Rivières horses were much too fast for the local competition. They were taking all the money, right up to what was supposed to have been the grand event, a race between St. Andrews' and Trois-Rivières' two best. And right then Jules, who was broke and thus sober, stepped into the middle of the track and blew a large unscheduled blast on his bugle, followed by an announcement bellowed in French patois that these Trois-Rivières horses were not worth a damn. He pointed to Trois-Rivières' finest and shouted, "Look at that plug. I'll bet he weighs ten times as much as I do, but he can't go twice as fast. And he's got twice as many feet to boot."

"You want to race him?" shouted the driver. There was a roar of drunken laughter from the stands.

"Sure I'll race him," Jules announced. "He's got all those extra feet and size, so he ought to go around the track five times while I go once, but if you put that nag five times around there wouldn't be enough of him left to sell to a glue

factory. So he goes twice while I go once. And I'll bet you a month's pay I beat him."

"I'll take you," called the driver. "Anyone else want to bet?"

No such sums of money had ever been laid on the line or pledged with IOUs in all of St. Andrews' history. Everyone in the stand was going to be rich or busted within a matter of minutes.

"You got to take off your shoes," insisted the sulky driver. "My horse ain't got no shoes on."

"What do you mean he ain't got no shoes on? What are those iron things under his hooves? Our man runs in his bare feet, you got to take them iron shoes off that jughead," shouted someone in the stands.

"It's okay," hollered Jules, pulling off his lumberjack boots. "I'll run in my bare feet. That hayburner can wear galoshes for all I give a damn."

The stands were empty as a thousand people clustered close to the starting line.

"That little maniac can have the pole," yelled the driver. "He won't have it long."

They were off, full tilt down the track, going with all the stops out. A mile and a quarter . . . Jules was holding nothing in reserve. He tossed his jacket aside, then his shirt. If he'd had time he would have removed his pants.

The horse was far ahead of him, a small speck way down the track. Then it came around and passed right at the half-way mark. Faster and faster Jules ran. Now his lungs began to hurt and his legs grew heavier with every stride. He'd never make it. He was going to let all his family and neighbors down. He stumbled and slowed a bit, and his lungs felt like bursting.

"Jules!" a voice cried. "Come on, Jules!"

From out of nowhere a car had appeared and was running off the track beside him. The car was the tow truck from the garage, and standing in the back was a man with a full quart of whiskey held high in one hand, the other pointing to it. "All for you if you win," he shouted.

That was what did it. Jules swore he ran the last four hundred yards without breathing. He crossed the finish line a yard ahead of the horse.

That night the town barroom did the largest business in its thirty-seven years of history, and Jules, then a young man in his early twenties, finished the entire bottle of Canadian Club and was well into another when he slid off his seat and slept the sleep of a conquering hero curled up beneath the table.

If you are a trotting enthusiast who doubts this story, someday stop in the St. Andrews bar, and there you will see a picture of Jules in the middle of a long row of photographs of famous trotters. And under it the title: LE CHAMPION 1902.

৯৯৯ Brush
Bottle and Fly

Luis Jansen was not related to us, but we Warner young were brought up to call him Uncle Luis. He had been my father's closest friend since he and Father met in the first grade in an Oregon public school and learned that they were of the same mind— they would rather hunt and fish than eat, not to mention a well-developed preference for the former sports over going to school.

Uncle Luis, when he wasn't in pursuit of quail, antelope, trout, or salmon, made a poor livelihood as an artist. While my father was becoming an engineer at Cornell, Uncle Luis studied art in Paris. He was not a great painter, but he was a good one, and certainly one of the best recorders of Western

American Indians that our country has produced. But his output was very limited. His trouble was that he would have started a painting of a squaw making a basket when her brave would suggest that they take off for a few days after trout, deer, or goats. The trout or the game would be brought in, but the painting somehow would never get finished.

Uncle Luis's unbusinesslike attitude annoyed my father, but not enough so that Father didn't help to support him and his wife, and not enough so that Father didn't continue to hunt and fish with him whenever he could get away from his business.

Uncle Luis should have married an Indian girl, but he didn't. Instead he met a girl in the Paris art school, who was nine parts witch and completely devoid of talent, and married her because she was the only girl around who spoke English. He started regretting this error the first day of his honeymoon and continued to regret it as long as he lived. Some women may occasionally nag, but Alice nagged from the moment she opened her eyes until she closed them at night. And Father said that he always suspected she nagged in her sleep.

My parents tried to persuade Uncle Luis to divorce her— Father even offered to finance a settlement— but Uncle Luis said no, and took his rod and bottle and headed for the nearest stream. A divorce sounded like too much trouble, and as the years passed he became pretty well inured to the nagging. He smiled benignly and seldom heard a word Alice yelled at him, and she had so many things to nag about that she seldom noticed his indifference. She just bounced from one of his faults to the next, and the more she did it the more inclined he was to wander over the hills with bottle, rod, or gun.

Occasionally he would paint an oil or watercolor, and if he

didn't send it to Father as a gift, Father would see it in Uncle Luis's home and insist on buying it for four or five times its value. Finally a respectable measure of recognition came to Uncle Luis in addition to Father's sincere appreciation. The Director of the Museum of Natural History came to our Long Island home for dinner and saw the Jansen paintings which Father had acquired. The upshot was that Uncle Luis came east at the museum's expense and in spite of his age— he was in his sixties then— a contract was drawn up and signed and Uncle Luis agreed to produce all of the backdrop paintings for the museum's American Indian Hall. The contract was a generous one, and we were all full of enthusiasm. At long last this man we loved was going to acquire a bit of fame.

Alas, we underrated Alice. Before his first mural was half done, her nagging drove him out of the house and off to his favorite river with his rod and a jug of mountain dew.

Uncle Luis was a superb fly fisherman, careful and loaded with knowledge of the rivers he fished. So when he reached the water's edge on this particular day he didn't plow in and start casting a dry or a wet fly. For quite a while he sat on a rock above the big pool he was going to work and observed the insect life on the river's surface. There was little of it, and the trout, if any, were leaving it undisturbed. Then he walked upstream a few rods and with a small pocket net searched the water for dead flies and living nymphs. He dumped the contents of the net into his hand and removed the leaves, twigs, and debris. All that remained were four tiny nymphs, an insect Uncle Luis had never seen before in more than fifty-five years of fishing. He studied one of the nymphs a long time, then tossed them all back into the river.

From one of the innumerable fly boxes he carried he selected a wet fly on a #16 hook. The fly had a dark-green chenille body, gray wings, and a generous amount of gray hackles below the head and two long wisps of pheasant feathers to form the tail. Carefully, Uncle Luis cut off the wings and trimmed the shoulder hackles down to almost nothing. The long tail feathers he left intact. Then he tied on a leader tapering to 4×, the smallest in existence at that time, put on the newly created nymph, walked twenty feet into the woods, away from the stream, and downstream to below the pool's tail.

For the past month a monster rainbow had dwelt in this pool— Uncle Luis had seen it four times beneath the surface of the clear water by standing on a high bluff and looking down.

When he reached the spot where he would wade in, he took a pint bottle from his pocket, sat on the bank, and poured out nearly half of it, filling a wooden cup he had carved from a tree burl for just such emergencies as this. He drank. It was a beautiful day and good, very good indeed, to be alive and here by this deep lovely river pitting his skill against that of a trout. Finally he finished his drink, nearly eight ounces of straight bourbon, and got to his feet and waded cautiously up to his hips in the water. He realized that he wasn't as steady on his feet as he might have been, but what the hell, he wasn't as young as he might have been either. Besides, if he couldn't wade when a little drunk, who could?

There was nothing the matter with his casting. He knew where the big rainbow lay, right where it had been each time he had seen it, in a deep pocket close to the bottom halfway up the pool, and off the end of a large dead tree that had fallen in a couple of years ago, out from the bank. There was no way he could persuade the trout to move into brush-free water. It would have to be taken where it was or not at all, and he would have to take his chances with the forest of branches beneath the surface.

He false-cast, stripping off line until he had about eighty feet of line and leader in the air, then cast. The nymph settled on the surface six feet above where the trout lay, and the leader curled toward the other bank, so the nymph would sink and go by the trout without the leader putting it down. Seconds later there was a barely perceptible twitch to that part of the leader that still floated. Uncle Luis raised his rod tip and was fast to the huge rainbow.

The trout did not dive under the branches, as he had feared it would, but went straight up the pool into water without a single obstruction. If he could keep it there, away from that cursed tree . . . The rainbow jumped. It was big, even for an Atlantic salmon or sea-run steelhead; for a rainbow it was enormous. Uncle Luis wished he had taken a chance of putting it down with $2 \times$ or $1 \times$ leader instead of this tiny tippet, hardly stronger than a thread. But there was no way to change the leader now. And if he could bring this fish to net on a $4 \times$ leader . . .

He waded upstream and out into deeper water, hoping to get around the tree. Finally the water was up above his lower ribs, and seconds later it started flowing down over the tops of his waders and the branches of the tree still jutted out four feet beyond him. The drop-off now was sharp, and he knew he would be swimming at least a yard before he went around the tree. Trying to swim in waterlogged waders . . . he would never make it.

He must play the fish where he stood and when it came downstream hope that it would be tired out and that with his rod tip he could swing it around the branches into the clear water below, where he would have an excellent chance to net it. If only the trout would stay upstream until it was beaten. . . .

For a long while the rainbow obliged. It raced back and forth in the clear water. Twice again it jumped, sending shivers of anticipation down Uncle Luis' spine. Uncle Luis, not a religious man, began to pray that he might keep the fish where it was until it rolled on its side and he could ease it by the tree.

His prayer was not answered. Slowly, deliberately, the trout moved down, a foot, two feet, a yard. There was nothing he could do to stop it. He knew the fish was tired— he must have had it on for nearly twenty minutes— but, wise old fisherman that he was, he realized that it still had a rush or two left and that if it chose to go under the tree he couldn't stop it. He stripped line from the reel, giving the trout free rein, hoping this would send it back upstream. But it didn't. The trout kept on moving down, not against the far bank, as Uncle Luis hoped, but in close to the bank with the tree.

When the fish was almost on top of him— he could see it right below him now— he started jumping up and down in his water-filled waders, thrashing about to scare the trout. Two things happened almost simultaneously. The frightened fish made a bolt in under the branches, and Uncle Luis lost his balance and went under, almost to the bottom of the pool. He tried to regain his footing and stand, but he was pinned down by the branches. They seemed to be everywhere. The more he struggled the more firmly they held him down.

Finally he ceased to struggle and gave up. He lay there, his efforts ended, quietly drowning in the pool. In the clear water he could see the trout, not more than a couple of feet away.

The line must have gone around a small branch that gave with the trout's pulls, and the trout was too tired to give a yank and free the hook or snap the leader. Uncle Luis reached out his hand and gently slid it along the trout's back until he clamped his fingers in its gills. At least they would be found together. Perhaps a world's record rainbow . . .

"For God's sake, wake up," Alice shouted. "What are you doing asleep at three o'clock in the afternoon? And wipe that damned grin off your face."

The smile remained on his lips. The grin seemed to Alice to widen. Suddenly she put her hand on his cold brow. She screamed. He continued to lie there, that happy look of deep content on his dead face.

That was a long while ago. My younger brother and I, all that are left of the family now, had decades ago forgotten Uncle Luis until a few months ago when we received a letter from a Southwestern museum director asking us if we had any of Luis Jansen's paintings and, if so, would we have colored photographs made as a book on his work was in preparation. And if we wanted to sell some of them . . .

Most of them we had long since given away to children, nephews, and nieces. We did our best. We sent names and addresses along, not knowing whether the generation behind ours owned them still or had passed them on as gifts to others.

I wrote to the museum director and told him that all I had was a hand-painted Christmas card to the Warner family, nine by twelve inches. The center is a water color showing a man with a fly rod paddling a boat that resembles an Indian dugout. In the background is a snow-covered landscape of trees and a small log cabin by the shore. In the lower right-hand corner Uncle Luis wrote, in a beautiful hand, "Christmas Greeting to the Warner family. 1894 Luis Jansen." In the up-

per left-hand corner there is a hand-printed verse from *As You Like It:*

> And this, our life,
> Exempt from public
> haunt
> Finds tongues in trees
> sermons in stones,
> Books in the running
> brooks
> And good in
> Everything.

$\text{\textit{ɷɷ}}$ Famous International Fisherman

A month or two after we moved to Washington, Connecticut, nine years ago, I received a phone call from a female who announced that she was a reporter on the Watertown *Sentinel* and she would like to come and interview me.

"What for?" I asked.

"I understand that you are a famous fisherman— that you have fished all over the world and write fishing stories for the magazines," she said.

"Well . . ." I began to feel pretty important.

That afternoon at four the lady turned up. She was full of business— lots of pads and pencils. She looked about old enough to have graduated from high school that morning. She was what is called in the newspaper business a stringer. Apparently the Watertown *Sentinel* did not consider my new home town its principal fount of news.

She sat down on the library sofa, dropped all her pencils on the floor, retrieved them, and asked, "What countries have you fished in?"

We were off, from Argentina to Australia.

An hour later she had run out of questions and I had run out of things to say. She had covered pages and pages that I hoped she could decipher, because it was a cinch no one else could. Sylvia brought in a tea tray. The young lady tried to help, and twenty pages of notes slid off her lap. As she picked them up in helter-skelter order, some pages right side up, others upside down, and none of them numbered, I was glad they were her notes and not mine.

Sylvia went off to try and find a picture of me that had been taken since World War II, and preferably in fishing clothes. Two days later the picture and story appeared under the modest headline: FAMOUS INTERNATIONAL FISHERMAN SETTLES IN WASHINGTON. The piece was incredible, even assuming that the typesetter was a Russian spy out to nail the paper's hide to the wall. The story had me catching hundred-pound tarpon in a Lebanese trout brook and battling it out with a ninety-pound brown trout on the saltwater flats of southern Mexico. Also, she became a little confused on dates, so I caught my first fish on a fly two years before I was born.

"My God!" I said to Sylvia. "I hope no one reads this."

She laughed. "Pity they didn't put it on page one instead of page two. Picture's nice, though, isn't it? You look as if you'd just climbed over the wall at Sing Sing. No, just tunneled under it." She whistled. "Boy! Are you going to be famous!"

I groaned. "Let's move to another state."

A week later Sylvia was downtown and a large man in a

house painter's uniform introduced himself as Whitey Anderson. He said, "I read that story about your husband. He sure knows how to fish, doesn't he?"

Sylvia said, "I am afraid the reporter got a little mixed up. For instance, there aren't any Atlantic salmon in the tanks of Ceylon, and I have never heard of anyone catching a smallmouth bass of fifty pounds. That last one should have been a striper taken off Cuttyhunk, and the Lord knows what the salmon should have been."

Whitey was paying no attention. He said, "We got a real nice trout stream in this town, the Shepaug. No one is allowed to fish it except residents of Washington. And the two fishing clubs here stock it every spring. Opening day is next Saturday. My brother-in-law, Oz Downes— he read that story too— and I were wondering if maybe your husband wouldn't like to fly-fish with us Saturday morning. Don't worry, we'll keep well out of his way. We'd just like to watch him."

Sylvia said, "Of course he'd like to go. And don't get carried away by that crazy story, he probably doesn't fish any better than you do. So please don't just watch him. Treat him like any other slightly demented human who thinks that God made the world only to keep fish on."

Again Whitey was paying no attention. "Tell him Oz and I'll stop by at five-thirty in the morning. Oz and I've been fishing the Shepaug going on thirty years, so we have a pretty good idea of where the trout are. And don't worry, we won't bother your husband at all."

Then Sylvia made what turned out to be two very bad errors. First, she accepted the invitation on my behalf. Second, she forgot to tell me until two a.m. on the morning I was slated to go, when I came back from a college-reunion party three sheets to the wind.

To say that I was not in good shape when she made the announcement would be the understatement of all time. And three hours later when she shook me awake I wasn't much better. No undertaker could have looked at me without licking his chops and starting to figure coffin sizes.

I started the day with two Alka-Seltzer tablets and three cups of black coffee. Then a horn honked in the darkness and I staggered forth to defend the honor of my home, and to meet Whitey and Oz. I wished there was some way I could swap heads with one of them. They told me that we would fish a place called the Clam Shell where you just walked down the bank to the stream, fished around in a circle, and wound up about where you had started.

Maybe if I lay down on the bank and stuck my head under water . . .

"Here we are," said Whitey. "There's the river."

At first I didn't see it because I didn't look straight down. But there it was all right, right at the bottom of a hill that made a ski jump look like flat land.

I said, "You fellows are all set up. You go ahead. I have to put my rod up and tie a new leader." I didn't have to tie a new leader, but it seemed like a swell excuse to get them started. I planned to shinny down that bank slow-motion while those two guys, who looked as rugged as mountain goats, would, I was sure, take it in a series of jumps out into space.

"No hurry, we'll wait," Oz Downes said.

"Sure, we've got lots of time," Whitey added.

So, having a dozen extra leaders in my fishing jacket, I tied another one. Ever tried tying a barrel knot with your head on upside down? Then I set up my rod, said a short prayer, and took my head down the precipice. I faced the hill and went down inch by inch, grabbing hold of every tree.

We made it finally— that is, I made it finally and found them sitting at the stream's edge having a smoke. I glanced back up the hill and wondered how I would ever get back up to the top. Maybe Sylvia could arrange to have a helicopter come and get me. Preferably one with a stretcher.

"Now you start right here," Whitey said. "There are some damned good pools the next quarter of a mile. Oz and I will start as far downstream as you can see. We'll fish dry and work up toward you. When we meet we'll take you to the best pool on the whole stream. There are generally at least a couple of big browns in there."

I watched them go, then stretched out on a flat rock and put my head under water. The water was ice-cold, and it helped. As long as I moved with the speed of glue flowing uphill my head felt, for the first time that day, as if it was only twice as big as the rest of me.

I fished slowly downstream with all the skill of a six-year-old trying the sport for the first time. Every few minutes I stopped and redunked my head. Trout? I couldn't have caught a trout if one had floated by me upside down. And I wasn't thinking about trout anyway. My problem was to survive and get back home to some more Alka-Seltzers.

Suddenly, as I climbed the bank to remove my fly from a bush for the umpteenth time, I was aware of my companions. There they sat, about fifty feet below me, smoking their pipes and watching my every move. What a treat it must have been for them— like going to hear a famous violinist play only to learn he's never had a fiddle in his hands before.

"How'd you make out?" Whitey asked. Before I could think of an answer to that one he added, "Oz and I both got our limits, so we quit."

At that time the limit was five per fisherman. Tempted as I was to announce that I had caught sixteen and thrown them all back, I was aware that fishing upstream they could have seen my every move, including any fish I did or didn't catch. I wondered if they had seen the FAMOUS INTERNATIONAL FISH-ERMAN dunking his head. Had they noticed that he'd gotten tangled up with every bush along the stream? Had they counted the number of times he'd had to stop to remove knots in his leader? "Beautiful river," I said. Nonchalantly I cast and hooked another bush.

"Nothing much right here," Oz said. "Let's go down to the big pool and see if you can't pick up a three-pounder."

By the time we reached their big pool I was as winded as if I had just run a four-minute mile. Also, my head needed re-dunking and I couldn't bring myself to do it in front of them.

"Right above where that bush leans out over the water is a pretty likely place," Whitey informed me. "Cast close as you can to the bush, then work your fly up five or six feet."

The bush was seventy feet, at least, below me, and right then I was in no shape to make an accurate seventy-foot cast. Hell! If I'd been sitting in a bathtub I couldn't have cast to the faucet without wrapping my leader around it.

So I did the logical thing. I stepped boldly forth down-stream, placed my felt-bottomed wader shoe on a rock that gave a bit, and the next thing I knew my head was again under water with all the rest of me. At least my head felt better.

I scrambled ashore with Oz and Whitey assisting, lay on my back, and raised my legs to let a few gallons of icewater run out of my waders.

Oz and Whitey were perfect gentlemen. They acted as though it happened every day. Whitey said, "That bottom is very treacherous. I should have warned you."

Oz said, "Getting along in the morning. Perhaps we'd bet-ter start up the hill."

There is nothing like a quick plunge in freezing-cold water to help a man climb a hill. Right then, for a hot shower and a towel I would have scrambled up to the top of Everest. Once I made it I waited as patiently as a man dying of the cold could for Whitey and Oz to finish the ascent.

Two weeks later, when I was almost over the flu, I went down to our local jeweler, John Benson, to get my watch fixed. I had invented a fine story as to how it had gotten full of water.

John inspected the watch and listened gravely to my story of forgetting to take it off in the shower. He said, "It'll take two weeks. A lot of water in there. Say, how do you like our Shepaug? Suppose it isn't much compared to some of those rivers you've fished."

Later I learned that John is related to Oz Downes. So that wasn't so bad. But a week later I drove ninety miles into New York and lunched at the Theodore Gordon Flyfishers. Thank goodness there would be no problem there, since, so far as I knew, I was the only member within thirty miles of Washington.

Dave Ogden, an old friend, said, "Hi, Bob. I want you to meet a guest of mine, Charley Keyes. Charley, this is Bob Warner."

Charley looked at me and a broad grin spread from one side of his face to the other. "Say, aren't you the famous international fisherman who fell in the Shepaug?"

I sucked in a deep breath. "How in hell did you know?" I asked.

He grinned. "I'm pretty famous too. Three days after you took your plunge I pried a four-pound brown out from under that bush you were trying to reach. I was with a guy named Oz Downes."